# Legal Practice Transformation Post-COVID-19

**Authors**
Jonathan Fortnam and Stuart Weinstein

**Managing director**
Sian O'Neill

*Legal Practice Transformation Post-COVID-19*
**is published by**

Globe Law and Business Ltd
3 Mylor Close
Horsell
Woking
Surrey GU21 4DD
United Kingdom
Tel: +44 20 3745 4770
www.globelawandbusiness.com

*Legal Practice Transformation Post-COVID-19*

ISBN 9781787425064
EPUB ISBN 9781787425071
Adobe PDF ISBN 9781787425088
Mobi ISBN 9781787425095

# Table of contents

# Introduction

This Special Report imagines how legal teams will operate in the post-COVID-19 environment.

Our use of the word 'team' is intentional: lawyers operate in teams. Whether as part of a firm, in collaboration with lawyers from other organisations or places, or as sole practitioners in a room at home in a small town in the United States, all rely on others to serve their clients. Those others can be third-party software providers, other lawyers, practice support staff, IT professionals, specialist consultants in forensics, accounting or project management and more: the list is growing almost daily, and our awareness of those others has been heightened during the COVID-19 pandemic.

Of course, teams can be anchored within law firms and this Special Report is primarily aimed at such an audience. But these teams usually include lawyers who practise in other environments:

- We have seen the rise in influence and prestige in the role of in-house legal counsel in organisations large and small worldwide. According to the Solicitors Regulation Authority (SRA), in-house solicitors represent around 17% of all solicitors, of whom:
  - 66% work in the private sector (in areas such as commerce and industry);

  - 27% work in the public sector (in areas such as local government and the Crown Prosecution Service (CPS)); and
  - 7% work in other sectors (in areas such as advice centres, charities and education).[1]
- As evidenced by the SRA's data on solicitors in the public sector and the CPS, lawyers play a critical role in the functioning of national, regional and local government, in roles that go beyond the conduct of litigation.
- Lawyers now practise in a variety of alternative business structures which allow non-lawyers to have a financial stake in the provision of legal services. These multi-disciplinary practices involve lawyers offering their services alongside accountants, conveyancers, mortgage brokers or insurance agents, who operate out of the same legal entity.
- Others trained in law or qualified as lawyers may work in fields allied to law or have portfolio roles that encompass legal responsibilities (eg, compliance officer, company secretary, head of governance or human resources officer).

Each group will operate in and contribute to legal teams for projects, cases and transactions, as well as day-to-day advice, governance and leadership across all aspects of the organisations we serve. And our success is interdependent on those with whom we work in teams. As such, in this Special Report, we speak in terms of legal teams.

Moreover, when we think of law firms, we also need to think beyond traditional law firm hierarchies (eg, partner, non-partner lawyer, other fee-earning roles and non-legal staff) and law firm geographies (eg, operating in different locations in one country or across multiples jurisdictions). We also need to envision how a single law firm may provide many different services, ranging from traditional lawyering to added-value services driven by new technology, alternative delivery centres and other forms of innovation. Thus, there are new models of organisations and new services to deliver; but always in teams.

If the successfully functioning legal team is the measure by which quality legal services are to be delivered, we could survey how legal teams have been operating during the COVID-19 pandemic and consider how legal teams have been affected. In a sense, this task would have been easier than what we are undertaking in this volume. Everyone knows the story of how legal teams moved out of their offices and into their homes for the duration; but as yet, there is no clear exit path from 'working from home for the time being'. For most legal teams operating in the COVID-19 age, the focus on near-term survival has passed; so now that it looks as though the worst is over, they can start imagining what the 'new normal' might look like.

What we do not yet know, however, is the full effect of the pandemic on the types of transactions that will take place or the litigation that will emerge. COVID-19 turned up winners and losers: aviation, oil and gas and travel being clear losers; pharma, online delivery services and supermarkets being clear winners. While we know how things are panning out at the present time, we do not know what to expect once children can return to school permanently, the scaffolding of government support is removed from industries and individuals, and a reckoning takes place of the effects of the pandemic on distressed industries and government tax coffers. This Special Report therefore imagines a post-COVID-19 world for legal services and asks what has changed, what has stayed the same and what values are critical that will endure in the successful operation of legal teams in the post-pandemic age. We do so in the following ways:

- Chapter I reviews some of the transformational changes that legal practice is facing, which have been accelerated by COVID-19. The pandemic is a moment of reckoning for legal teams, in that it has become clear that there is an urgent need to invest wisely to ensure the seamless delivery of legal services through digital platforms.
- Chapter II explores the 'psychic harm' done to lawyers and their teams by being forced to work from home indefinitely. Not only has this led to dislocation and confusion, but the loss of separation between 'work' and 'home' has brought new challenges and will require a different mindset if this is to become a fixture of legal life post-pandemic.
- Chapter III scans the horizon to evaluate what work in legal teams might look like once we return to the office after the pandemic. This chapter involves making some 'uneducated guesses', because no one knows when, how or why we will be returning to those desks we abandoned in March 2020.
- Chapter IV explores issues of trust, which in the legal profession tend to centre on the requirement that lawyers act in a way that upholds public trust and confidence in the profession. Here we look inwards, focusing on building trust in a legal team faced with the complexity of working away from the office, when communication is only intentional and yet fragmented. For managers, the problem is particularly critical: how can they lead and model best practice when their contact with staff is intermediated 'through the looking glass' of Zoom or Microsoft Teams?
- Chapter V examines the financial picture for law firms that is emerging from the pandemic. The analysis looks at the balance sheet for partners when the downturn started in 2020 and what capital will be needed to prepare for when the economy 'bounces back' and pent-up demand once again stretches legal team resources.

- Chapter VI acknowledges that there is no guarantee that in the age of COVID-19, legal teams will be able to keep calm and carry on lawyering. While the pandemic has forced lawyers – who tend to be more analytical, deliberative and objective – to make decisions on gut instinct and to innovate and improvise on the fly, it is the long-cherished values and beliefs that encapsulate professionalism in the law that will see us through this difficult period, even if it feels like the brakes are coming off right now.

The authors would like to acknowledge the support of our commissioning editor, Katerina Menhennet, for her patience and humour in working with us throughout the process of moving from concept to finished manuscript.

This is the first publication to come from the business of law initiative at Aston Law School, which is focused on producing practice-informed research and insights into management and leadership in the legal sector.

Aston Law School is based in the heart of Birmingham (not far from Aston Villa FC). We hope that you will get in touch with us so that we can introduce our students, alumni and academic colleagues to you, to explore ways in which we can further this dialogue on the business of law.

# I. Different legal teams will have different solutions

**1. Rapid integration of digital technology in the delivery of legal services is the new 'killer app'**

We start with the hypothesis that the legal profession is in flux and that the changes already taking place have been heightened by COVID-19, in that the pandemic has accelerated certain developments. For instance, the trend towards virtual law firms that emerged before the pandemic continues, although it is likely that what was once an outlier has certainly become more mainstream. In short, availability in the legal profession has moved from an emphasis on location to logging in online.

The move to virtual practice is indicative of a transformation that is taking place in the delivery of legal services. Legal outputs such as drafted documents are no longer produced 'under one roof', but are undertaken, delivered and implemented through a digitised process 'in the cloud'. The use of automation platforms that operate across law firms, in-house legal departments and related professional advisers such as auditors, risk managers and integrated service platform consultants requires us to rethink the current legal working environment.

Instead of dividing the legal profession into the static business entities which lawyers have established in order to operate their enterprises, our assessment of the way in which legal professionals have been operating during the pandemic suggests that a realignment through digital technology is enabling lawyers and allied professionals to operate more efficiently across organisational boundaries.

COVID-19 has transformed how lawyers and clients communicate and interact with each other. While digital technology is a 'force multiplier' for the legal profession, in that it allows work to be completed more quickly, it also means that less time is spent travelling and commuting. COVID-19 has brought about a loss of community cohesion for the legal profession, in that digital technology does not allow for the sort of 'water cooler' talk that informal networking opportunities previously generated. The loss of spontaneous 'cheek by jowl' interactions outside the courtroom, in the pub and at networking lunches or continuing professional development events means that lawyers are now more isolated than ever.

While lawyers began to adjust to working in an environment in which there is less opportunity to consult with each other informally, COVID-19 also required that work get done within an accelerated timeframe. Lawyers had to scramble to meet the demands for a speedy response

*"A realignment through digital technology is enabling lawyers and allied professionals to operate more efficiently across organisational boundaries."*

in uncertain circumstances for which no precedents were readily available. The response times in such a crisis often needed to be instantaneous, as the situation was changing daily and there was thus less time for lawyers to reflect, consult and gather their thoughts.

Lawyers (or private practitioners, at least) who are more accustomed to looking back at precedent have had to advise on situations for which precedents simply do not exist. The lawyer's temptation to cover all angles has always been obsessive; yet during the pandemic, the angles have been changing all the time. So is the discomfort that lawyers are now feeling a good thing or a bad thing? Will it generate more creativity or lead only to more frustration? Is this a problem or a cause for celebration?

Technology and urgent challenges have forced the entire world, including the legal profession, to respond far more quickly than in the past. For example:

- COVID-19 vaccines were developed in less than a year, whereas previously such an endeavour would have taken years; and
- the Brexit trade deal between the European Union and the United Kingdom, which would normally have taken years to negotiate, was finalised in an eight-month period in 2020.

Likewise, COVID-19 required greater use of appropriate technology platforms to operate in different ways and adapt to the demand for a 'work from anywhere' environment. The business improvement cycle mandates behavioural change to keep lawyers effective and responsive to a crisis that has beset us all.

So the question becomes: how do lawyers interact with technology?

One solution might involve better change management: how can lawyers adapt to change to drive professional success?

Questions to ask of all legal team managers in the age of COVID-19 include the following:

- "Why are we doing this?"
- "What values does this bring to our organisation?"
- "Can we use COVID-19 to make changes in how people work together?"

The pandemic should be viewed as a moment of transformation, enabling the legal profession to change and practise creativity to survive and thrive.

## 2. The current state of play with legal practice

Outside of the law firm environment, legal teams have always been seen as a cost function of the business. Can technology make legal teams a more collaborative partner? The way we look at legal, as a sunken cost, is inherently problematic and the traditional legal structure highlights these issues. No longer can we distinguish between the lawyers and the business partners they work for – we are now all one team. Legal work is typically characterised by the entity that does the work. Work is done in-house, at a law firm or sometimes contracted out to a barrister in specific circumstances. Law firms typically handle 'high-impact' or 'enterprise-threatening' work; while in-house legal departments handle commoditised services that are too mundane in scope and not cost effective to hand over to private practitioners. For instance, litigation is generally handled through law firms. The projects that are ideally suited for in-house legal teams should typically be handled by someone with a long-term institutional memory or who is keenly aware of internal political sensitivities (eg, competitive fiefdoms, difficult personalities). Organisations are not dissimilar to families, in that they too do not want to air their dirty laundry in public – even to their trusted legal advisers.

The 'bricks and mortar' model of the legal services entity – whether part of a larger company or a standalone entity – has tended to be characterised by boundaries, structures and hierarchies. However, this is now giving way to new models that are more amorphous, at the behest of businesses and/or clients which are increasingly demanding that legal structures suit their specific needs and requirements – not the other way around. In the old days, clients simply adjusted to their lawyers' work environment: lawyers were put on a pedestal, not to be bothered except at special moments. Today, lawyers are fully involved in the 'sausage making', embedding legal concepts throughout the process from beginning to end.

- Project management is a key skill here. Getting to the end of a deal is just the beginning – think of on-boarding and off-boarding a dozen or so stakeholders in the process.
- Pragmatism is also crucial: you cannot say "No" as a lawyer when your business people must engage with hundreds of different processes and systems.
- New blood in the organisation – such as coders, project managers and IT people – can help; but budgets are stretched.

Whereas in the past, legal structures were defined by office hierarchies and compensation structures, today law firms are subject to an assault from flat hierarchies where form follows function. Thus, the delivery of legal services today can level out the players and has reduced, to a certain degree, the advantages of the traditional

*"Whereas in the past, legal structures were defined by office hierarchies and compensation structures, today law firms are subject to an assault from flat hierarchies where form follows function."*

hierarchies in the legal profession (eg, Magic Circle, Silver Circle). For instance, if a professional services firm (eg, one of the Big Four accounting firms) can gain an asymmetrical advantage over a top law firm by leveraging technology with lower cost overheads, it will win the business. Everyone wants to avoid a 'Kodak' or 'Nokia' moment, where your organisation becomes obsolete because it does not adapt to the market. Think of how Google Maps and the Uber ride-hailing app have devalued the much-vaunted 'Knowledge' of London black cab drivers. No one wants to be a dinosaur!

**3. Will we hire lawyers through an app?**

One cannot minimise the loss of the physical contact that typically characterised the operation of the legal profession pre-COVID 19. Traditionally, legal practice development depended on contacts and networking. Contacts require a certain degree of locality – the adage "all politics is local" is certainly applicable to the legal business. People generally hire lawyers or legal teams based on where they are located and who else they work with, and by referral. Law firms and barristers tend to situate themselves around the courts in which they appear. They also tend to locate in city centres, near the large financial institutions and companies that they advise. With lawyers and legal teams now isolated from the physical closeness facilitated by shared workspaces and the endless networking synergies available in metropolitan legal centres, can LinkedIn and firm websites bridge the gap?

While an online presence may help, it alone cannot 'seal the deal' like a handshake.

- Will COVID-19 do for the legal profession what Uber did to the ride hire business?
- Will the selection of legal counsel be determined by what an app pulls up?
- Will lawyers who are not included on these platforms lose business because they are not seen, so they cannot be heard?
- Will lawyering become more about how you access the lawyers you choose, rather than who they are and what their skillsets are?

**4. COVID-19 is a disruptive moment that favours challenger firms**
Prior to COVID-19, many large legal services established 'back-office' functions in second-tier UK cities or in other jurisdictions with lower cost overheads, such as India and South Africa, setting up local legal process outsourcing operations to carry out sophisticated work through digital platforms. The pandemic has increased the ability of smaller players to gain asymmetrical advantage against their more established competitors by adjusting quickly to uncertain market conditions through the development of innovative service delivery strategies. These challenger firms can act in an agile manner that larger, more established firms cannot match, as the latter face legacy issues with digital technology, high fixed costs (eg, premium commercial property leases) and other fixed overheads that do not adjust for reduced business volumes (eg, insurance coverage, utilities costs, subscription services, pension obligations).

Delays to in-person learning for children, the absence of available day care and increased redundancies at law firms and in in-house legal operations all mitigate towards the rise of virtual law offices, which can quickly act as a gap filler to address shortcomings in market demand and legal expertise capacity. Having your primary workspace at home and using shared office conference space on an 'as-needed' basis to meet with clients is no longer seen as second-best to a fully dedicated office space; the gig economy has transformed legal services as much as it has other service industries. The rise of nomad lawyers and 'lawyers on demand' (LODs) may worry some who feel that a lawyer who does not operate from a fixed support infrastructure base as a 'safety net' is someone who is risky to use. However, the perception that LODs are 'lawyers of nowhere' died a quick death once it became clear that we have all become nomads of some sort through remote working requirements.

Flexible legal services – such as those embodied in start-ups designed to match lawyers pursuing a portfolio career while working part time with clients in need of their services – have proven quite attractive for lawyers who 'want off the treadmill' to achieve a better work-life balance. This is not to say that the large law firm model is dead in the water after COVID-19. In fact, after a slower start in 2020, for many the year finished stronger than initially feared.

### 5. COVID-19 and the delivery of legal services through digital platforms

Just as streaming content providers such as Netflix, Amazon, Hulu, Showtime and HBO have transformed Hollywood, threatening the future of entertainment production and distribution, legal digital services platforms are upending the ways in which legal services are provided and delivered. Moreover, the ways in which clients access legal services and interact with their legal advisers will challenge traditional expectations on the preparation, delivery and implementation of legal advice and services.

Legal analysis involves grappling with hard questions for which there is often no one single correct answer; so while digital infrastructure will reduce costs and increase the speed and adaptability of the provision

*"The pandemic has increased the ability of smaller players to gain asymmetrical advantage against their more established competitors by adjusting quickly to uncertain market conditions through the development of innovative service delivery strategies."*

of legal advice, it will not supplant the judgement calls for which the best experts can charge serious fees that clients are willing to pay. Nonetheless, just as important as these professional judgement calls is the need for a universal collaborative platform through which legal advisers, their clients and IT service providers can exchange ideas and facilitate work solutions, with lower entry barriers than current subscription service platforms. The point here is not to reinvent the wheel, but rather to reimagine the wheel so that it is more egalitarian and open to all to share creative ideas and legal innovations.

### 6. The medium is the message – how legal services are delivered is becoming more important than who delivers them

In the 1960s, Canadian philosopher Marshall McLuhan wrote, on the impact of the mass medium of television, that "the medium is the message", and that the content delivered by this medium was subservient to the way in which it was delivered to the public.[2] The same can be said of the legal profession in the age of COVID-19. Law firms and their clients have already started to deliver routine products that are the result of collaborative services available through digital upscaling. One example of this is aosphere LLP, an affiliate of Allen & Overy, which provides cross-border online legal data for sophisticated but repetitive financial services transactions to more than 500 global institutions in integrative formats. COVID-19 has intensified the use of digitised information platforms as an optimal way to merge knowledge exchange with practice requirements in a manner that is tailored to the requirements for interfacing with legal professionals when different countries – and different regions within them – are faced with different levels of COVID-19 restrictions.

However, one area in which the medium is not the message is trial advocacy. Remote working in the context of appellate litigation is workable. This can be attested to by appellate lawyers Lisa S Blatt and Erica L Ross, who had the honour of being the first lawyers to argue a case this way in May 2020 before the US Supreme Court.[3] However, in the context of a trial, which requires cross-examination of witnesses and a jury to weigh testimony, there can be problems. For instance, it is nigh impossible to gain the sense of a courtroom from looking at disembodied faces on a computer monitor. Courts have wrestled with the important question of when the use of virtual courtrooms could result in unfairness to one of the parties to a case. In Australia, for instance, courts have ruled that cross-examination by video link may lead to unfairness where the demeanour of witnesses would be hard to gauge or where the case involved is a multi-party litigation involving complex issues for which witnesses are necessary to establish an appropriate context.

The development of legal function digital support tools can be used to

*"The development of legal function digital support tools can be used to integrate the law firm or legal department with the internal teams or external clients that it supports."*

integrate the law firm or legal department with the internal teams or external clients that it supports. Legal tech products that have cross-functional application within the entire organisation or that can be used directly by law firm clients can build a network of champions for the legal team across the organisation, or for the law firm within its client circle. An internally focused tool will not secure buy-in from those whose support the legal function or law firm needs most to ensure that its advice and counsel are implemented to the benefit of the client.

The shift in existing legal institutions – such as courts, government agencies, clients, law firms and in-house departments – towards functioning in a fully digitised manner is essentially continuing without regard to the pandemic. These legal institutions need to keep up with a society that is rapidly becoming digitised. For the legal profession, the benefits include time-saving reductions in labour-intensive operations. The development of real-time-based applications for legal risk analysis – equivalent to the Internet of Things, which has transformed manufacturing; or regtech, which is changing financial services – should be the logical next step for the management of legal risk.

- Stayin' alive: This is no longer a question of competitive advantage, but more likely a question of survival for today's lawyers and the legal businesses they advise. While no app will replace a lawyer, this is not the goal we should be aiming for when incorporating more tech into legal services. Some perspective is needed, and can be gained from looking at the automotive industry in 2021: while the latest car models may have self-driving features, none of them is self-driving. While it may be useful to bring coders with legal training into law firms and legal departments, an inexperienced individual with coding skills will not substitute for a lawyer with experience who can offer his or her judgement on legal issues.

- Keep it real: Trimming legal costs during a pandemic may not be wise in the long run if it is done in a hasty or poorly conceived manner. In any trimming of costs, one must identify the sacred cows that are at risk from new teams and new solutions.

**7. 'Legal teams', not 'law firms' + 'in-house' – the death of the siloed lawyer**

Talking transformation needs definition. Greater fluidity is needed in how we define 'law firms', 'in-house legal departments' and 'alternative legal service providers' in the current environment. Do these labels have value anymore? We need to look more closely at the substantive tasks performed – for example, what individuals do and how they align

> *"While it may be useful to bring coders with legal training into law firms and legal departments, an inexperienced individual with coding skills will not substitute for a lawyer with experience who can offer his or her judgement on legal issues."*

with other players – as opposed to where those tasks are performed. We would argue here that the term that should be used to describe the new way in which legal services are being provided, and will be provided, is 'legal team'. Responsibility is now held across different organisations and entities, and 'siloed' legal services are gone.

Even as we accept the idea that the 'siloed' legal team is a liability to the organisation it is a part of, how will individual lawyers avoid being 'siloed' if, following the pandemic, more of them work in isolated settings? Many reports suggest that people have worked harder in lockdown than they did when they commuted between home and office. The tabloid predictions that if people do not work in an office, they will 'skive off' have proved wide of the mark. Instead, it seems that many have worked harder in the sub-optimal world of lockdown, because this is seen as a temporary arrangement. However, what if this model – working from home – becomes the new normal?

As of January 2021, many of the big City law firms are looking at their footprint in terms of the high rents they pay for swathes of unused space in premier locations. This sounds reasonable in the context of a pandemic; but how does a law firm chief operating officer assess space needs that match the length of commercial leases, which range from 15 to 20 years in duration? It may be that post COVID-19, a new model of three days at home/two days in the office could replace the lockdown model of 100% work from home. Not everyone agrees, however; the trend Down Under is quite the opposite. "I'm not Robinson Crusoe in saying this – everyone is – but I really agree that it's just critical for our junior lawyers and grads that they be in and around the buzz [of the office], with its opportunities to learn directly and a little bit by osmosis from partners," says Gilbert + Tobin partner Simon Muys.[4]

### 8. Conclusion: reimagining the legal profession post-COVID-19

While we are fighting the pandemic, it is hard to gain perspective to envision what life-affirming steps we can take to reimagine the legal profession once we emerge from lockdown and COVID-19 is behind us in the rear-view mirror. If the enforced family time has made us better partners, parents and members of the 'sandwich generation', those benefits will inure to the legal profession in terms of the enhanced emotional intelligence that we will bring to our careers. For those of us who have lost loved ones to COVID-19 or who might ourselves be living with long COVID, our empathy skills and resilience have been forged in tragedy in a way that we could never have imagined before the onset of the pandemic. We have argued that the new model for the delivery of legal services involves lawyers embracing greater cross-functional skills that will enable them to provide better service in their specific legal discipline. To the extent that COVID-19 has made us better humans, we have added to the cross-functionality of the legal profession; and that is in and of itself a good thing – albeit an unquantifiable one.

This discussion has a built in-bias, in that seeking to improve the legal profession and the functioning of legal teams presupposes that what we had before the pandemic was 'normal', or an example of what was good or what should be replicated post-pandemic. But nothing could be further from the truth. When we compare the COVID-19 pandemic with other paradigm-shifting events in our lifetimes – the 2009 global financial crisis, 9/11, the 1978–1979 Winter of Discontent or the oil crisis of 1973 – we can see how each of these events transformed how we live, how we work and what we value and believe in, to enable a fundamental review of previously accepted norms.

If COVID-19 shines a light on practices in the legal profession that have been tolerated in the absence of the imagination, energy or imperative for alternatives, this could be a moment to bring about some positive outcomes. We hope that some of the solutions for the operation of legal teams post-COVID-19 proposed in this Special Report prove helpful to consider and a cause for reflection.

# II. Remote working is here to stay

### 1. Location, location

If an Englishperson's[5] home is their castle, what then was their office? Was the *office* in fact their castle: a place in which order (what's more, *their* version of order) existed; where people knew their place and knew the rules of the game? Indeed, if 'the office' was in fact an actual private office – and possibly a spacious one – its resident not only knew the rules of the game, but had also played the game and won.

In short, 'the office' was never just an office. That space on the second floor was never just the place where a lawyer worked; it was so much more.

If we start with the very location of an office, a quick dip into popular lawyer culture reminds us of its significance. As any follower of *Suits* will know, an office's size, view, proximity to reception and/or corner location served as a symbol of status earned via success in court, closure of the biggest deals (all involving the most extreme behaviour) and, of course, that 'go-to' measure of success: client billings.

Then there was the decoration. Art, sideboards, trophy basketballs, drinks cabinets (think of Harvey Specter's Macallan 18 whisky) – each spoke of the occupation or perhaps *possession* of a space; an esteemed space, a *personalised* space, where things (*important* things) happened. Hence, the residents of those spaces were demonstrably people who made important things happen in their way; they were winners and their named offices bore testimony to the fact. It was also a place to chat at the end of the day, to reflect on success and catastrophe; a place of safety, away from others.

It was the place where the majority of lawyers got the vast majority of their work done during (alas) the majority of their waking time. It was where work *stuff* was. More than desks and chairs (which also spoke to the status of their occupant), the tools of a lawyer's trade were to be found in the office. Shelves of books; cabinets of files; piles (and piles) of paper; latterly, desktop computers and printers – a lot of *stuff* that was considered necessary for work (a view which was not challenged) was located at the office. For while lawyers might have made their offices (or latterly, their own parts of the office) homelier in their decoration, work tended to be done only at the office. Indeed, it was difficult, if not impossible, to relocate all the stuff that one needed to work anywhere else, without perhaps hiring a removal firm.

Then there was the community of people needed to do the work. PAs, print room staff, fellow lawyers (colleagues, whether superiors, peers or juniors) – those people were also located at the office. It was good to work in teams and teams existed to work *in the office*. Everything that was necessary to make work happen on a long-term and sustainable basis was located *in the office.*

This also meant that junior lawyers and PAs *could* work. Typically living in more modest homes, these key workers would have had neither the space nor the facilities to work other than at the office. As before, the prospect of relocating PAs and support staff and what they needed in order to do their work was even more daunting than for lawyers. The equipment they used to work was part of the fabric of the place in which they did that work (well, almost). The notion of working elsewhere was not even a possibility for this vital cog in the legal team.

The office was also the place where others in the legal team (be they clients, counsel, e-disclosure providers, subcontractors or other professionals on a deal) met and worked together (even if by video or telephone conference, if not in person). The infrastructure to make this happen was located in the office. Of course, mobile phones, then personal digital assistants and now laptops and tablets made it much easier to work from home on an occasional basis. However, this increasingly powerful and resilient digital mobility was understood to facilitate an exception to the norm, an occasional arrangement; the tools enabled lawyers to work somewhere unusual for an unusual

*"It was good to work in teams and teams existed to work in the office. Everything that was necessary to make work happen on a long-term and sustainable basis was located in the office."*

part of their time (and only perhaps because they were winners at the office).[6]

*A lawyer's office was always much more than a place to work.*

Everyone who worked at the office was broadly happy that this was the case. They were happy to work (and work hard) at the office; to collaborate with colleagues at the office; or just to be at the office, to have access to their stuff and the stuff that they needed to work.

In short, the office delivered – it had to, and so it was trusted (and we will return to trust in a later chapter) and not questioned.

**2. Home sweet home**

By contrast, home was where work was not (or was not supposed to be). We measured our work-life (im)balance by time spent at a specific location. Time at the office was time away from home and vice versa. Time at home was the counterbalance to time at the office.

We must be careful to avoid stereotypes when describing home, as we know that home is not the sanctuary for all that it is for some. Let us paint two pictures, alternate perspectives perhaps, that will at least cover the bases. You can pick and mix to reflect your experience.

First, let us dip into the pages of an interior design magazine, where all is well. Here, home is a place of welcome, acceptance, safety; it is a personal space, in which our own personality, and the personalities of those we live with, can be explored and expressed without the relentless existential pressure to account for every six or so minutes. It is a place of community, in that we might share it with family and friends, with whom we enjoy spending time; a place where we share a mutually beneficial agenda that includes time for rest and recreation, and where we can work through the trials and conflict of life in an atmosphere of trust.

Next, let us imagine the letters page of a teenage magazine. Here, home is a place where there is conflict, as family members struggle to realise who they are and what role they occupy in the family and the world when they are exhausted after a day's labour; a place where emotions run high and are not understood, let alone accepted. Shared times are either boring, hard work or both. It is a community of rules that are lopsided; and let's not even go near trust...

Wherever you draw the line between these two scenarios (and they are not extremes), home has its own benefits and challenges; its own hopes and expectations; its own expressed and implied 'ways'. They

*"For now, remote working is here to stay; so lawyers must reimagine all that the office meant to the teams of which they were a part."*

are sometimes easy to navigate and at other times little short of gruelling. Like the office; and yet, not the office.

What is the point of this trip down amnesia lane in a Special Report that reflects on the impact of a global pandemic? It is to explore the dislocation and confusion that the pandemic has brought for thousands of UK lawyers and their legal teams. Lawyers who previously spent long and rewarding times at 'the office' have had to 'work from home', where work was not and where the other was.

### 3. All change!

When, on 16 March 2020, the UK government announced that all unnecessary social contact should cease, it ushered in the first period of lockdown, which for most UK lawyers meant the need to work from home – and not just for a day or two. This was a massive change for many – not just as a matter of logistics (much more than a new laptop for the kitchen table and a pair of headphones); rather, it was a *dislocation* – even a bereavement – of identity, community and utility. This was equally true for the senior lawyers embedded in their offices as for the digital natives who had grown up using technology and were famous for their connectivity, independent of time and location.

Initially, maybe, some of us did not miss the office. The weather was fine and the garden was a pleasant spot for lunch. In addition, lawyers were grateful to be busy (advising on *force majeure*, furlough and rent clauses), well and living with reduced risk from public transport and colleagues – although admittedly, with schools and nurseries shut, childcare was a challenge. But overall, the dislocation was either manageable or at least a price well worth paying. After all, we would soon be back to normal.

By the time of the second national lockdown in November 2020, the larger part of the legal community still had not returned to the office. Hearts and minds were still adjusting to new patterns of working that did not involve hours 'wasted' daily on an uncomfortable, unsafe commute. In addition, the institutions within which lawyers live, work and have their being, such as the courts, had moved their work online too. The centre of gravity seemed to have shifted. Subsequent lockdowns have solidified these transitions.

### 4. Change as a constant

So what of the office? What of the ecosystem it spawned and supported? What of the trusted systems of operation planted and nurtured in the office? Are we destined to no longer meet colleagues from the same legal team in the same room, instead inviting them along with strangers into our homes via MS Teams?

These are big questions, and we are still in the early days of responding to the pandemic. For now, remote working is here to stay; so lawyers must reimagine all that the office meant to the teams of which they were a part.

In the next section, we seek to capture some of the headlines of this reimagining in the form of a table and then start to explore how we might make some progress.

## 5. Change as an opportunity

### Table 1. Defining the working environment

| The office is a place of ... | Working from home is a place of... | Working online can be... |
|---|---|---|
| Status and safety | Stretch and insecurity | Democratic and engaging |
| Work and achievement | Struggle and getting by | Distinctive and reinventive |
| Collaboration and community | Dislocation and distance | Without boundaries |
| Trust | Abandonment and ambiguity | See later (!) |

Perhaps the first point to note is the change in terminology: locations are dead; long live online. The point is one of more than semantics. For the reasons we have touched upon, we need to acknowledge that online working often requires that we welcome each other into our homes; but this is no longer how we should define the experience. Work is work, wherever and however it is undertaken. And there are benefits to working online: colleagues prevented from attending the office by their location (due to distance or confinement) can benefit from a level playing field with their more local and mobile counterparts. We have to embrace online working; let us also make a point to celebrate its opportunities.

Next, we have already acknowledged the office's contribution to our sense of status and safety. Working from home, on the other hand, has been a dislocation that has stretched the usual proxies of order. This can give rise to insecurity in a number of respects. First, what if, as a junior lawyer, you cannot reach your supervisor and have a client deadline to hit? And more objectively, what about the technology and the availability of confidential and privileged information? Lawyers must be trained to manage these commodities in new deregulated environments (there is seldom a key code on the door to the spare room).

The future might be a place of democracy/equality, where project management skills will be at a premium. This is not to say that planning timed contributions is always necessary. However, for structured engagement, it will be a necessary development. Levelling the hierarchies of office accommodation might also help junior lawyers to become more confident in their participation in meetings and discussions. Less obvious and more direct engagement is likely to be an opportunity welcomed (no more obviously closed-door discussions). And if working online means the end of office gossip, perhaps this might be an unintended but pleasant benefit of this massive dislocation.

### 6. Change as a threat

"You're on mute". "Can you hear me?". "Is that better?". "Apologies – we are having some technical difficulties". My fellow lawyers, enough is enough. Before the pandemic, we would not have tolerated locked meeting rooms; starting meetings with only a few attendees seated

*"Levelling the hierarchies of office accommodation might also help junior lawyers to become more confident in their participation in meetings and discussions."*

*"We achieve more in collaboration and community. However, most lawyers are trained, from undergraduate level onwards, to work individually and competitively."*

and with no access to pens and paper. The time has come for us all to become fluent in the technology of remote working. Familiarity is not enough; we need fluency. Not in every application or each aspect of functionality; but email, document production (both of which should look more like professional outputs and less like ransom notes) and video calls (from setting up to sharing screens and managing chat) are core skills and frankly, there are no excuses to the contrary.

If we are not serious about this, we risk creating digital ghettos of disenfranchised teams and individuals. Digital competency has become a matter of reputation (and not a chargeable activity). We suggest an audit of kit and capability, leading to a gap analysis and, if appropriate, immediate training and/or support.

Also, be aware of your team's FOMO.[7] Information and comfort that they may previously have picked up in the office will potentially be lost to them when working remotely. So regular communications are mandatory. Whether by email or a short video clip, think of predictably good ways to communicate so that the team knows what is going on (and what is not).

Think also about working without the usual signals for the passage of time. With commuting time becoming computing time, and no office cleaner, last train or prospect of another office-based pizza to announce the end of the working day, it is possible to work many hours without being noticed. Short-term attraction becomes unsustainable habit in the medium term and damage in the longer term. We must discover ways of noticing the weary and overburdened. The infrastructure that perpetuates unsustainable hours is under challenge. But the skills that make for good lawyers cast their shadow in life more generally (see Professor Laura Empson's work on 'insecure overachievers').[8] So maybe this is the time to move away from chargeable hours as a way of valuing lawyers' work and measuring their success. Fixed pricing promotes efficiency; it recognises the ability to focus on outputs rather hitting chargeable hour targets and has the potential to drive proportionate working practices. Further development of this theme is beyond the scope of this Special Report. But for now, what better opportunity to change the metrics and the harmful narrative that a lawyer's contribution is measured by their stamina rather than their insight and ability to cut to the chase?

It is perhaps worth remembering that no one became a lawyer by being work-shy. So why do many traditional approaches to valuing lawyers' work seem to forget this?

Let us celebrate lawyers' outputs and client outcomes, get client feedback and maybe think about default maximum chargeable hour limits (rather than targets).

### 7. Change as a force for good

We also know that we achieve more in collaboration and community. However, most lawyers are trained, from undergraduate level onwards, to work individually and competitively. Times are changing and clients are using their buying power – at least implicitly – to champion a different way. As noted, the paradox of the early days of isolation was that lawyers found community 'in the same boat' and were forced to collaborate as we developed the new status quo. However, old habits die hard and it will not be long before collaboration at a distance is found in the 'too difficult' pile.

So also think about transparency in your communities. During the first few days and weeks of the pandemic, plans for even the short-term future needed to be reviewed daily or even hourly. We might soon find ourselves in what Warren Bennis and Burt Nanus named a VUCA environment. 'VUCA' stands for volatility, uncertainty, complexity and ambiguity. It was the response of the US Army War College to the collapse of the Soviet Union in the early 1990s. Suddenly, there was no longer a single enemy, resulting in new ways of seeing and reacting.[9] We need to be ready for a VUCA world. Avoid debating possible responses to future contingencies and focus on today's decisions.

Then communicate them. Be user oriented and tech savvy in the means of communication – email is not always best, especially when people have been starved of human contact and time is short.

Don't forget the social side of meetings. The personal catch-up on arrival, when tidying and gathering up, on departing; the chance to hang back to ask for 'a minute' – all are lost in a digital, back-to-back world. Make time. If we click to leave the meeting as soon as the agenda has been concluded, we miss catching up on news of the children, the football and (of course) the weather – not just for its own value, but also as a proxy for proximity, the glue of community cohesion. Be intentional about the discussion. Encourage openness and develop accountability.

As the world vaccinates against the pandemic, we might expect a blended composition of working practice (in reality, mostly online) to become the norm. The key to success will be for legal teams to identify and incorporate the positive habits and developments of an exclusively online environment into a blended existence. To this end, let us take care to identify and avoid the consequences of working from home and embrace the opportunities of working online.

# III. Health and safety for legal teams post-COVID-19 – uneducated guesses?

**1. Nobody knows what the return to work for legal teams will look like**

All of us have had our lives upended by COVID-19 – whether we have lost a loved one, been infected ourselves or avoided the virus only to have to assume complicated roles in our families, sandwiched between caring for parents who are shielding and children who are struggling with the challenge of learning by webcam. While we all hope for that 'magic moment' when we all come out of lockdown and leave our isolation bubbles, and life returns to normal, the reality will be a lot more challenging. In *Ode to the West Wind*, first published in 1820, Percy Bysshe Shelley wrote: "The trumpet of a prophecy!
O Wind, if Winter comes, can Spring be far behind?"

Can the same be said of the return to the office for lawyers? If the virus is beaten, will we go back to work in the same way we did before the pandemic? Or rather, will our work lives be shattered irrevocably after COVID-19?

We do not pretend to have a crystal ball that can predict what will happen to the world of work once the worst of the pandemic is over. However, we think that certain trends and patterns can be observed that may govern the working environment of legal teams post-COVID-19.

**2. "You must work from home if you can"**

These words from the UK government have shaped our life since March 2020. If someone is unable to work from home and can work safely in their place of work, they can do so provided that their workplace remains open. However, the subset of people who cannot work from home has been very limited since the UK government abandoned its ill-conceived 'back to the office' campaign in early September 2020. Without any irony intended, lawyers by and large do not fall within the UK government's category of 'essential workers'. As such, for most lawyers and the legal teams in which they work, working from home has been – and will remain for some time – the default position.

In the face of COVID-19, employers will have to think long and hard about how to require staff to return to the workplace. People have grown accustomed to the alternative arrangements now in place, which meet most of the needs of those who work on legal projects. However, one question that remains unanswered is whether, post-COVID-19, the government will push hard with another 'back to the office' campaign, like it did at the end of Summer 2020, which was fatally ill-conceived. Many legal employers, if left to their own devices, might be more inclined to permit some of their employees to work from home on a regular basis once the emergency has ceased.

This is a far more sensitive issue than people realise. The youngest justice of the UK Supreme Court is a spry 58 and the oldest is 73. This spread of ages reflects the fact that age is less of a limiting factor in the law than in other professions. For instance, the Honourable Jack B Weinstein, a US district judge in Brooklyn, New York who was appointed by President Lyndon Johnson in 1967, finally entered inactive retired status at the age of 99 on 10 February 2020.

Will legal eagles and those who work with them whose age and/or health conditions may require them to continue to shield feel pressure to return to the office even though herd immunity through the mass vaccination roll-out may not yet have been fully achieved? And what should we do with those team members who will not stay at home, even though we may have concerns that they should? Can a manager order an employee to stay at home in such a scenario? How should this 'order to stay away' be handled such that it is considered a reasonable request made on a non-discriminatory basis?

The fact that the largest workplace outbreak of COVID-19 in the United Kingdom took place at the Swansea offices of the Driver and Vehicle Licensing Agency (DVLA) does not augur well for the UK government's ability to properly manage a safe return to work. Some employees at the DVLA claimed that people with symptoms were encouraged to return to work, while vulnerable workers had requests to work from home turned down.[10]

- What if a member of a legal team feels it is unsafe for them to return to work?
- Will employees who cannot return due to continue shielding requirements be the first to be laid off if redundancies are necessary?

The adage "out of sight, out of mind" resonates when we think of the challenges that those who might be unable to work in an office environment post COVID-19 may face. No sensible employer could, for example, require pregnant employees to work in frontline roles, even once a mass vaccination campaign is complete, until a longitudinal study of the risks has been conducted. The British Medical Association (BMA) also points to current evidence (as of January 2021) which shows that those from an ethnic minority background, those of Filipino birth and those who are older have been disproportionately affected by COVID-19, with specific underlying conditions increasing the risk of severe illness. In addition, being male has been associated with more severe cases of the disease.[11] What will legal teams do to ensure that these people do not become invisible in the post-COVID-19 workplace?

*"Employers will have to think long and hard about how to require staff to return to the workplace. People have grown accustomed to the alternative arrangements now in place."*

There is anecdotal evidence of COVID-19 forcing older workers into early retirement. While many of these individuals may have contributed to legal teams in non-legal roles (eg, working in the café, attending to reception or working in other support functions), the damage done to inter-generational teams by the sudden departure of individuals over the age of 55 with co-morbidity factors such as cancer, chronic kidney disease or heart disease, who could not work from home, is an unpleasant reminder that COVID-19 is cruel. Now that we have vaccines, it remains to be seen whether some of these co-workers who contributed so much to the workplace will return. If they don't, the post-pandemic work environment for legal teams will be worse off for having lost these much-valued older workers.

### 3. COVID-19, difficult conversations and unspoken bias

When the pandemic ends, legal teams will have to work hard to avoid bias against hiring and retaining older lawyers for fear that a future pandemic may sideline them. Some scenarios to consider include the following.

#### Mr B QC

- Solicitors need to retain a silk to act as counsel for a company in a complex fraud litigation to take place at the Royal Courts of Justice, London. It is likely that the trial will take place up to two years from now.
- The company is presented with the bios of two QCs who are qualified to take on the file: a 55-year-old female, Miss A QC; and a 68-year-old male, Mr B QC.
- The company's chief executive has expressed a preference to hire Miss A QC, as she is not in the higher-risk categories for contracting COVID-19, as opposed to Mr B QC.

#### *Analysis*

- Mr B QC might have a direct discrimination case.
- Mr B QC could argue that he is being treated worse than another person (Miss A QC) because:
  - he has a protected characteristic;
  - the chief executive of the company thinks that he has that protected characteristic (known as discrimination by perception);
  - his circumstances are such that that they are sufficiently similar to those of Miss A QC, who is being treated better, for a valid comparison to be made; and
  - the discrimination was unlawful in that the treatment happened in a situation covered by the Equality Act 2010 (ie, the receipt of services).
- The company could argue that treating Mr B QC differently due to his age may be allowed if it can show that there is an

*"When the pandemic ends, legal teams will have to work hard to avoid bias against hiring and retaining older lawyers for fear that a future pandemic may sideline them."*

objective justification (eg, a good reason) for this difference in treatment. To rely on the objective justification defence, the company must show that its policy or age-based rule is for a good reason – that is, "a proportionate means of achieving a legitimate aim":

- A legitimate aim must be a real, objective consideration and not in itself discriminatory (eg, ensuring the health and safety of others is a legitimate aim); and the importance of this legitimate aim must outweigh the discriminatory effects of the unfavourable treatment.
- Additionally, no alternative measures must be available that would meet the aim without too much difficulty while avoiding such a discriminatory effect.
- If proportionate alternative steps could have been taken (eg, working in tandem with a junior), there is unlikely to be a good reason for the policy or age-based rule.

- As there is no objective justification for treating Mr B QC worse due to his protected characteristic, this would constitute unlawful direct discrimination, despite the fact that the company may have some reason for it.

### Solicitor C

- The economy has picked up substantially, with vaccine take-up in Asia, Australia and New Zealand, North America and Europe (including the United Kingdom) so high as to achieve the requisite herd immunity in these regions.
- A major multinational based in New York wishes to retain a Magic Circle firm to assist it in acquiring the telecommunications network of a multinational with major operations in Africa and Latin America, where vaccine roll-out has been slow and herd immunity is still some way off.
- The due diligence requires a leading telecommunications legal team to visit operations on both continents together with the investment bankers, to ascertain in person the value of these ongoing operations and the licences and liabilities they hold in the various jurisdictions in which they operate.
- The Magic Circle firm has two potential experts to lead the team and conduct the due diligence visits: a 35-year old male with a history of diabetes and obesity (Solicitor C); and a 45-year-old female with no known conditions that could lead to an increased likelihood of severe illness from COVID-19 (Solicitor D).
- Solicitor D is chosen by the managing partner to lead the transaction and do the necessary travelling. The firm's insurance coverage would not cover Solicitor C if he contracted COVID-19 during his travels for work; as such, there is no question that Solicitor D must staff this transaction.

#### *Analysis*

- Solicitor C might have a case for indirect discrimination.
- Here, the firm has a travel policy that applies to the entire workforce, but that disadvantages people who share a protected characteristic: susceptibility to COVID-19 due to health conditions.
- Solicitor C is disadvantaged as a member of this group.
- In applying this policy, the firm must demonstrate that there is a good reason for the policy.
- In these circumstances, whether anyone intended Solicitor C to be disadvantaged is not relevant.
- The case for indirect discrimination is as follows:
  - The insurance policy and accompanying travel policy apply equally to all at the firm.
  - The policy disadvantages people who are susceptible to COVID-19 due to pre-existing health conditions.
  - These pre-existing health conditions are protected characteristics.
  - Solicitor C may show that the policy has disadvantaged him personally.
- However, the firm may show that there is a good reason for

applying the policy despite the level of disadvantage to people with protected characteristics.
- Thus, in this circumstance, the organisation can show that there is an objective justification which may overcome the claim for indirect discrimination.

### Fee Earner E

- You are the managing partner of a law firm and you discover that one of your fee earners (Fee Earner E) is very active in a COVID-19 denial group.
- You find out that a couple of weeks ago, Fee Earner E was arrested along with a group of other individuals for engaging in an illegal protest in violation of lockdown restrictions at a major London hospital.
- Fee Earner E is strident in his belief that COVID-19 is a hoax and is writing blog pieces and doing interviews expressing his views to the press, which is starting to offend clients of the firm.
- You take Fee Earner E aside for a heart-to-heart about his COVID-19 denialism activities, which you believe are interfering with his work and are offending some of the firm's clients. In response, he explains to you that COVID-19 denialism is his belief and is a protected characteristic under equality and human rights law, because it affects his life choices and the way he lives.

#### *Analysis*

- Two prongs of analysis must be considered here:
  - Fee Earner E claims discrimination by perception because he holds a particular philosophical belief: 'COVID-19 denial'.
  - Fee Earner E claims that his activities – writing blog pieces and doing interviews expressing his views to the press – connect him to individuals who have similar beliefs about COVID-19, so this is discrimination by association.
- As managing partner, you have no views concerning Fee Earner E's beliefs and activities, even though they are unpopular with clients.
- However, if Fee Earner E's presence at the illegal protest in violation of lockdown requirements at a major London hospital crossed the line, resulting in a criminal conviction, the firm must terminate Fee Earner E's employment, as his conduct contravened firm policy in respect of appropriate conduct outside of work hours.

### Partner F

- A partner at the law firm (Partner F) came down with COVID-19 during the first lockdown. She was hospitalised and spent a protracted period in intensive care.

- While the firm is happy that Partner F is back at work on an adjusted workload considering her recovery, clients are noticing that her work is not what it was prior to her contracting COVID-19. Some clients are beginning to ask that she not be staffed on their matters.
- You want to talk with Partner F to see if she is suffering from long COVID; however, this is a difficult conversation which you would prefer not to have.

*Analysis*

- You should revisit the situation whereby Partner F is working with reasonable adjustments to see whether the firm can better support her.
- Examples of best practice in dealing with employees affected by long COVID include increasing the professional staff support available to them (eg, having a personal assistant to work with them to ensure that deadlines are being met and appointments are kept as scheduled).
- A meeting is held with occupational health, at which Partner F receives counselling and undergoes cognitive impairment evaluation appropriate to individuals suffering from long COVID, such that an individualised support programme can be developed to assist her with her long-term recovery.

### Legal Team Member G

- The legal department has managed to make the transition to working from home reasonably successfully.
- Internal clients of the legal department are happy with turnaround times and with the responsiveness of most team members to the needs of the sales and marketing group, which is the biggest client of the internal legal staff.
- You notice that one member of your team, Legal Team Member G, is missing scheduled Zoom meetings with colleagues in sales and marketing.
- Moreover, colleagues in the legal team note that Legal Team Member G never uses the webcam when communicating with colleagues on MS Teams.
- You are concerned that this staff member is suffering from depression due to social distancing and self-isolating.

*Analysis*

- First, you need to look at what steps you can take to catch up with Legal Team Member G to see whether she is coping well at this time.
- In an open-ended conversation, see whether you can steer Legal Team Member G to workplace mental health support, such as an employee assistance programme helpline, counselling services

or peer support groups which may be available, including pairing her up with another colleague who will check in regularly to see how she is doing.

The examples outlined above require deft managerial skills, legal knowledge, emotional maturity and empathy to address them in a manner that is consistent with the desirable attributes of the legal profession. We like to think that as guardians of the legal profession, we have a responsibility to maintain a safe, welcoming environment in which individuals can achieve their very best, professionally and personally. However, we need to be realistic that getting the balance right in the age of COVID-19 and its aftermath is no easy task.

### 4. Glimmers of hope: will 'work from work' be something special and different from 'work from home'?[12]

Like all crises, the COVID-19 pandemic will pass in time, but its impact in the longer term – from both a societal and an economic perspective – is likely to be profound. Prior to COVID-19, many of us saw the daily commute as a grind to be endured, which was stressful, costly and unpleasant. Rail travel in the United Kingdom is expensive. A season ticket from St Albans City to London St Pancras costs £3,936 per annum; from Milton Keynes to London central terminals costs £5,360 per annum. Add to this misery congestion charges in London and Birmingham, equally high parking fees (when spaces can be found) and one-mile taxi fares of between £6.20 and £9.60 in London, and one cannot help but feel a bit of *schadenfreude* at the misery that commercial landlords are experiencing in attempting to convince the hordes of office workers that made them wealthier from rentier capitalism to return.

'Work from work' will have to be made special. People will come back to offices only if what is on offer to them from working in city centres is more advantageous than remaining at home. The crucial factor, of course, is getting children back to education on a regular basis. Nothing can be done until the stop-start way in which schools have been operating in the United Kingdom since March 2020 is ended. The schism between the children of 'essential workers', who can attend school, and all other children who are currently being home schooled highlights that any plan for a mass return to offices will not be achieved until those who work with children have received their COVID-19 vaccinations.

When one considers that in the United Kingdom, it costs on average about £233 to retain a registered childminder to care for a child under the age of two for 50 hours a week, one quickly realises that working from work is a very expensive proposition for many households. Admittedly, some of the issues raised here concerning the cost of childcare in the United Kingdom (which typically ranks first or second highest in most global surveys) mitigate against the gender equality gap, which is a critical issue in the legal profession, as women comprise most entrants to law school and the legal profession.

One year into the pandemic, if 'work from work' means a brutal commute into and out of a city centre, paying £8 for a cappuccino and a baguette at a train station and enduring the threat of recurrent breakouts of COVID-19 variants, it is a non-starter. Commercial landlords will have to offer more than discounted rents to law firms and big companies to get them to stay in city centres. What is the offer for the typical worker that will entice them back to city developments such as Canary Wharf? A long-term relationship with these returning office workers that offers something of real value other than what they could get by remaining at home will be necessary to revitalise the 'work from work' culture. It may be, for instance, that 'work for work' proves more attractive to those under the age of 45, who will want to get back to the pubs and experience city nightlife; but those over the age of 45 who (having already spent up to 25 years commuting into work) will have real concerns about flocking back onto crowded trains and the London Underground, and about the risks of encountering super-spreaders on public transport or in the workplace.

*"The reality is that people will not go back to working in offices like they did before the pandemic. The UK government, commercial landlords, retailers and transport providers will need to adjust their horizons to the new reality."*

### 5. Grief for what was lost

The office culture that existed in urban centres prior to 2020 is just one of several aspects of UK life that have fallen by the wayside in the age of the pandemic. Socialising in pubs, attending live theatre and going to football or rugby matches have stopped for now – and some may never return. As the days passed in March 2020, it soon became apparent that everything had changed; but the UK government still failed to realise that the music had stopped. Perhaps the starkest illustration of this was its insistence that the Cheltenham Festival go ahead notwithstanding the rise of the pandemic across Europe, bringing 150,000 racegoers to Cheltenham racecourse just days before lockdown measures were eventually introduced. The UK government was caught flatfooted once again in August 2020 when it launched its ill-fated 'back to the office' campaign, only to call it off shortly thereafter due to rising infection rates.

The reality is that people will not go back to working in offices like they did before the pandemic. The UK government, commercial landlords, retailers and transport providers will need to adjust their horizons to the new reality. 'Work from home' has shown us that people realise there is less need for each of us to travel to city centres every day to get work done. While there are advantages to face-to-face contact and to meeting in person and as teams, there is a realisation that far less contact with others in person as opposed to electronically will characterise the years to come.

We really do not know what the magical point of herd immunity is but until it is achieved, all talk of returning to the office is pure fantasy. This problem is heightened by the existence of variants which have had a negative impact on immune responses in laboratory tests; and also by vaccine hesitancy, which is hindering take-up of the COVID-19 vaccine in some segments of society.[13]

### 6. The unasked question is now asked: can UK employers mandate COVID-19 vaccines for employees?

Professional services teams, such as those working in law firms or in-house, have been shown to be fully capable of working from home during the COVID-19 pandemic. As such, there is little evidence to suggest that mandatory vaccines would qualify as a reasonable instruction for members of legal teams to follow. While the case for mandatory vaccines in the social care sector, the police, prisons and the National Health Service (NHS) makes complete sense and can be justified as necessary, these arguments make less sense in the legal services sector, unless an organisation regularly deals with vulnerable people who are at risk. For instance, while a mandatory vaccination policy might make sense for the CPS, the National Probation Service or HM Courts & Tribunals, it would be hard to justify for corporate

*"It is far more sensible for employers to encourage voluntary vaccinations for staff and let Parliament take the lead on mandating vaccines where needed as events develop."*

law firms. Each organisation is different and will have to weigh the pros and cons of adopting a mandatory vaccination stance. Unions will need to be consulted in those legal teams where such a position might be appropriate or advisable.

And even if you decide that it would be a reasonable instruction to require the employees in your legal team to take the COVID-19 vaccination, what is the likelihood that employees could be dismissed for failure to follow such a reasonable vaccination instruction? The answer: very slim.

Although employers may dismiss individuals fairly on the pretext of a dismissal for some other substantial reason, the very requirement for a vaccine would become an issue of contention and employees would likely litigate to challenge whether the requirement and the instructions given were reasonable and appropriate.

It is far more sensible for employers to encourage voluntary vaccinations for staff and let Parliament take the lead on mandating vaccines where needed as events develop. This is especially true in light of the new variants that are regularly arriving on the scene, against which current vaccines may not offer adequate protection.

### 7. Legal teams after COVID-19 – trauma and transformation

We have discussed in this chapter how the transition to 'work from home' has in turn transformed 'work from work' in the legal profession. Our focus has been on the United Kingdom, where the authors are based. However, the reality is that the health and safety risk for legal teams after COVID-19 pales into significance when compared to that faced by other teams which have had to bear the full brunt of the pandemic day to day.

On 28 January 2021, Lynsey Addario – an award-winning photojournalist with expertise in covering war zones – wrote in the *New York Times*:

> *I recognize the trauma I see in frontline workers, battling to maintain life and dignity in a situation of mounting horror. Though the vaccine – which has reached over seven million people in Britain – is a light at the end of the tunnel, the darkness of what the country has experienced must not be forgotten.*[14]

Addario is right.

To a remarkable extent, the pandemic has spared legal teams, in that we have not suffered the losses that NHS and other frontline workers have borne. We have been able to go about our work lives with inconvenience, but less disruption and very little risk to our own health.

We owe the workers who experienced with their own eyes the awful trauma of the COVID-19 crisis our unbounded gratitude for what they did for us so that we could proceed with our lives as normally as possible.

# IV. Culture and community

### 1. "Trust me, I'm a lawyer"

We have already touched on the importance of maintaining community elsewhere. We would now like to develop that thinking in this chapter, recognising as we do the importance of trust to our culture and community.

Trust is axiomatic to lawyers. Our clients trust us with their business secrets and sometimes their personal secrets; the law itself imposes obligations on lawyers that support the notion that we are to be trusted. An obvious example is that communications between solicitor and client in the context of legal advice are protected by the law of privilege.

So why then do our internal work practices and norms suggest the opposite?

In 2003, Robert Galford and Anne Drapeau[15] described the challenges of building trust within an organisation, comparing this to the demands of a management consultant (and perhaps their thinking extends to any 'trusted adviser', such as a lawyer):

> *It takes more than personal integrity to build a trusting, trustworthy organization. It takes skills, smart supporting processes, and*

*unwavering attention on the part of top managers. Trust within an organization is far more complicated and fragile than trust between, say, a consultant and a client. With a client, you can largely control the flow of communication. In an organization, people are bombarded with multiple, often contradictory, messages every day. With a client, you can agree on desired outcomes up front. In an organization, different groups have different and often conflicting goals. With a client, you know if there is a problem. In an organization, there is a good chance you do not, even if you're in charge. If things are not working out with a client, either party can walk away. That is not usually an option for people in an organization, so they stick around. But if they think the organization acted in bad faith, they will rarely forgive – and they'll never forget.*

Galford and Trapeau's insight is profound and perhaps explains the management challenges that beset busy client-oriented legal teams. Legal teams are used to managing or perhaps controlling client relationships, and the successes of those relationships might not be replicated within the 'home' team. That is for another day. The point for now is that building trust in an organisation is difficult enough when it is possible for the leadership and management to engage in face-to-face communication and be observed in what they are doing. It seems to be more difficult in a legal team. Add the complexity of working away from the office – when communication is only intentional, and yet fragmented in the sense of its 'stop-start' rhythm – and it becomes doubly difficult. Then add the fact that leadership cannot be observed outside of the managed meeting – neither leadership nor their teams are in a position to pick up the vibes, to see the smiles and to assess the authenticity of what is being said and written – and it is clear that maintaining and cultivating trust become very challenging indeed.

As most leaders know, when engagement – both visible and audible – lapses (or is perceived to lapse), team members (and teams) will fill in (and confirm) the gaps themselves; and this is not always done in a positive way.

The final sentence of the extract from Galford and Trapeau's work is significant. It is not only when organisations act in bad faith that trust is eroded; it is also when the team *thinks* that is how the organisation has acted. Note what then happens: the writers suggest that trust is lost –possibly forever. When leaders and their managers are out of sight, when communications come from a distance, the risk of misunderstanding is magnified many times over. Trust is a fragile commodity that is under attack.

## 2. Trust under attack

Leaders of legal teams would be right to recognise that, in addition to people and infrastructure, trust also formerly resided at the office. Once dislocated from the office, trust – to the extent that it was ever present – is at risk.

In their bestselling book, *The Five Dysfunctions of a Team*,[16] Patrick Lencioni and Kensuke Okabayashi identified the absence of trust as the first indication of dysfunction. Kathryn Peterson, the fictional Datatec's new CEO, reminded her board: "[T]eamwork begins by building trust. And the only way to do that is to overcome our need for invulnerability." Vulnerability is a difficult quality to share in the most conducive of environments; but outside of the office, it is especially difficult to communicate accurately. Teams that have worked together well in what we now know to be a conventional setting might have a chance of maintaining trust online. But what about new team members and new teams? What about the way in which we launch new projects?

You see, historically (by which we mean, 'until recently'!), 'outside of the office' was usually mistrusted:

*"As most leaders know, when engagement – both visible and audible – lapses (or is perceived to lapse), team members (and teams) will fill in (and confirm) the gaps themselves; and this is not always done in a positive way."*

- We might remember the partner or senior lawyer who habitually 'worked from home' (cue knowing smiles and nods) on Fridays, especially during the summer months, and the erosion of trust that involved. Reports on the recording of chargeable hours were never quite the same when they came from someone who 'worked from home', irrespective of how busy they were. This was a case of *trust eroded.*
- In time, a day spent working at home to get a report done or to finish a witness statement became acceptable, provided that the deal was honoured. If the report appeared in circumstances where it might not have otherwise done following a day working from home, then the (perceived) leap of trust (and the dislocation of the normal) was rewarded. This was a case of *trust on condition.*
- Increased agility and the roll-out of mobile IT (laptops and enhanced technical literacy (although not yet fluency)) to all lawyers gave rise to working from home for convenience, as opposed to necessity. A home delivery or repair justified a day working from home, rather than the sacrifice of a day's leave. There was less of a need (or perhaps no need) for a deal to be struck (*trust on condition*). Yet, as with its forerunners, a day away from the office was a *different* day – an unusual day; and

*"Traditionally, trust within legal teams seems to have been based on a 'line of sight' in the office. There are possible reasons for this, but they need to be seen for what they are."*

while it was tolerated with varying degrees of equanimity, it was an exception to the norm. This was maybe a case of *trust strained*.

- In the early days, working from home on a regular basis was treated as an option for those not on the partner track, with an implied sexism that it was primarily reserved for early to mid-career women with childcare commitments.

At least the government's decision to lock down on 16 March 2020 meant that law managers did not have to decide to close their offices themselves. The lockdown came swiftly and soon every day resembled the Sundays that many of us knew as children. All but the most essential shops were shuttered, and the reward for those who managed to get into those outlets that opened was often empty shelves. The trust dynamic of the office was pushed to one side in favour of survival – not just as working lawyers (we were initially busy (and therefore happy) advising on the consequences of the lockdown, such as *force majeure*, rent payments and furlough entitlements). In the early days, survival was more about us as humans and as general communities, as opposed to business teams – that came later. Was this *trust suspended*?

### 2.1 Let us pause and reflect

- Trust is important – both for our relationships with clients and across legal teams. It is built into our role and is a specific responsibility for lawyers in what we do.
- Traditionally, trust within legal teams seems to have been based on a 'line of sight' in the office. There are possible reasons for this, but they need to be seen for what they are.
- In recent pre-COVID-19 times, trust developed materially to accommodate occasional or even regular, but not usual, working *away from the office*. But that is the point – it was away from the office, defined by what it was not: somewhere else; not somewhere in its own right; not a positive place that could be trusted completely. We had to explain where we were.
- COVID-19 challenged that by forcing legal teams to relocate to home at pace. And it worked. We now realise that our dislocation could be more than temporary – it could be, perhaps, to some extent, forever.[17] Hasty introductions to MS Teams and Zoom, which had previously avoided the mainstream spotlight, have gone well and the tools are now (mostly!) trusted by all.
- Legal teams and lawyers need to rediscover trust in the one-dimensional environment of online working, where we meet only by appointment and where there is no chance simply to observe a manner or absorb a sense. We can no longer meet in the office kitchen; instead, we invite each other into our own kitchens. We need to do what is long

overdue: to recalibrate what trust looks like and build it out – deeper and stronger than before.

## 3. Trust rediscovered

Let us look at a few ideas as to how we as leaders might go about this, and how this is a team effort in which we might just have to think a little more like insightful adults and a little less like lawyers.

Frances X Frei and Anne Morriss wrote that leadership is a combination of authenticity, logic and empathy.[18] We look at each of these elements in turn below. They need not necessarily be applied serially; although there is an obvious logic and attraction to what Vanguard describes as the 'check, plan, do' approach that is premised on the idea that if you know the 'what and why' of current performance, you will have confidence in planning and executing change – which may be distinguished from the lawyer's natural instinct to 'plan, do and check'.[19]

### 3.1 Authenticity

This is so important: doing what we say, walking the talk and being authentic are of fundamental importance. Authenticity is a starting point in the sense that without it, everything else that comes afterwards – no matter how good – is undermined; potentially terminally so. Authenticity is perhaps better thought of as an overriding necessity, which must be continually reinforced (remember our WFH Friday partner?). Here are some thoughts to start with:

- Admit to the challenges: There is no use pretending, we are in difficult times. Some things are better than others, but not meeting at all is likely to be difficult for most of us. Admit it! Working in a place where work is not can be difficult for most of us. Admit it! Admit it and start to deal with it. And maybe share how: this will inspire trust and confidence. The days of invincible leaders in 'command-and-control' mode have gone. In a VUCA world, we need more than one mind on any subject and we need to be adaptable. If this is a threat to your self-image as a leader, move over.
- Practical difficulties: These will also need attention. Dealing with them (and doing so well) will be a proxy for institutional trust. So proper IT and effective IT security in the WFH environment are important. If there are gaps in this provision, let your teams know that steps to remedy the situation are underway. Teams should be aware of the need for and limits of IT security. If it has been a while since the last round of IT and cybersecurity training, then it's time to refresh.
- Confidentiality: This is also important to manage. Ask your team whether they have any concerns and whether steps can be

*"The days of invincible leaders in 'command-and-control' mode have gone. In a VUCA world, we need more than one mind on any subject and we need to be adaptable."*

taken to support them as they maintain client confidentiality. There may need to be some investment and some creativity here. A while ago, there was talk (gossip) of one firm that offered a loan to employees to pay for the construction of a garden office; but a screen filter might be enough. Otherwise, what about out-of-town spaces for employees to dock in?

- Home versus work: Knowing when to stop without the usual prompts is a challenge. Stay in touch with your people and ask specifically how they are managing. Be prepared to share what works for you (and be sensitive to your situation compared to those of others). Model both the challenges and the solutions.
- Realism: Be realistic in your decision-making agenda. If the situation is changing (as it was almost daily at the start of the first lockdown), decide only what you must when you can (and meet regularly). Do not spend time planning for eventualities that are unlikely to happen; it wastes time and introduces unnecessary complexity.

### 3.2 Logic

The predictability of good decisions is a real strength to a leadership team in times of crisis. Good decisions come from an informed, 'real-time' understanding of your own situation and those of your stakeholders. Do not leave this to chance and do not depend on impression or sense alone; our leadership lens may distort the truth and be insufficiently reliable. We are aware of the perils of information overload so interestingly highlighted by Malcolm Gladwell in his fascinating book, *Blink: The Power of Thinking without Thinking*.[20] The introduction (titled "The Statue That Didn't Look Right") serves to illustrate the point, as it contrasts the accuracy of an informed glance compared to 14 months of expert analysis and scientific investigation by the J Paul Getty Museum prior to spending some $10 million on what was thought to be a marble statue from the 6th century BC. It is important to audit (or just ask) as part of the 'check' of 'check, plan, do'. Being authentic increases your chance of getting honest answers; be aware that certain team members (not always the more junior) will say what they think you want to hear.

- Do not be satisfied with the first answer. Also, think about making an impromptu call to see how members of your team are doing. The chance conversation in the lift or the coffee queue will not happen in lockdown; you need to recreate it (without surprise – remember, they can't see your face when you make the invitation).
- Be systematic about asking how your team are getting on and remember that the point of the call is not necessarily a social

*"Wanting to be part of the solution rather than part of the problem (eg, by insisting on a fee) is significant in demonstrating and building trust."*

one. At our university, we instituted a concerted effort to speak with every staff member during lockdown ('contactless contact'). Some conversations were less than we might have hoped for in terms of human warmth and humour. Nevertheless, that did not matter. When we surveyed the staff later in the summer, an overwhelming percentage said anonymously that they highly appreciated the support they had received. These calls are not 'social', in the sense that the aim is not to deepen friendships; instead, they are appropriate leadership actions to show that we care. Friendship and care are not the same! Good leaders care, full stop.

- Take time to check in with your stakeholders – the communities on which your legal team's success depends:
  - Think of *their* triple bottom line (but do not show off about it): ask about the issues facing their people, profit and 'planet'.
  - What have your stakeholders lost? How are they struggling? Your success depends on them (and their clients/customers); so do not just think about your legal team's direct clients – think also about *their* clients/customers.
  - Do not boast about caring: this is not a marketing strategy! It is part of being in business – an investment in a relationship that may not translate immediately into instructions and fees. Hang in there; wanting to be part of the solution rather than part of the problem (eg, by insisting on a fee) is significant in demonstrating and building trust. If you do not, there could be bigger challenges around the corner.
- Get on the front foot with your legal team, to remind them of the team's purpose and strategy statements. These should serve as their 'North Star' – the principles that guide them through stormy seas as well as calm waters:
  - How are the business and the teams that you lead and serve shaping up against their *raison d'être*?
  - If you are a general counsel, is there a need to speak truth to power to stay true to the purpose of your business? We believe in the value of a purpose (and research shows that purpose-led businesses perform better in the longer term than their competitors).[21] So focus on your purpose and, if appropriate, encourage your team members to discover and follow theirs. This should not be a 'programme' or an 'initiative'; those speak of a driven business. There is both need and opportunity for legal teams which are led in ways that afford individuals the space and permission to connect with the reason why.
  - Be intentional and lead in ways that people want to (and do) *follow*.[22] It may not be enough to wait for clients to dictate the innovation strategy. We are accustomed (even pre-

conditioned) to following our clients' lead; but let's not substitute service for laziness or, more likely, an unhealthy excess of caution. At a time when many of the familiar aspects of professional life have been dismantled or side-lined, there is space and time for us all to remember *why* we are who we are: *why* we are lawyers; *why* we are in the team. Let's rediscover the *whys* and discuss them. The COVID-19 dislocation might also allow for an honesty that familiarity can mask.[23]
    - When other teams are focusing on consolidation, there may be opportunities for those that look outwards. There will certainly be some when the lockdowns are over – and better to have a rolling start than a standing start.
- Check that you are acting in ways that are consistent with your leadership ambition. If you are not sure whether you are, ask a colleague to watch and read what you say, do and write. Also, have a think about:
    - actively approaching decision making in new ways that are 'Zoom friendly';
    - making time for chats – start meetings 15 minutes early and/or finish earlier (15 minutes before the new hour), so that there is time for what GPs call the 'door-handle conversation'.[24] This is sometimes the most significant moment of the colleague's day – the moment to share something that has been bugging them for a while; and
    - exploring the technology beyond simple utility. Be aware that software is developing in response to new working arrangements and patterns. Might breakout/networking rooms be used to recreate the relational glue that holds our rough edges together?

### 3.3 Empathy

Remember that not everyone has the same physical infrastructure in which to work.

Many of the senior voices who described a smooth transition from the physical office to a dislocated digital existence had their own office environment at home. (Interestingly, their workplaces were decorated to be homelier, while at least part of their homes was designed to be more office-like.) And yes, we all know far too much about former British Prime Minister David Cameron's 'man cave' – the rich person's version of an 'office away from an office'. But junior members of the team are unlikely to have the same provision: lockdown in a one-bedroom flat, working at a counter or a small table in the kitchen, will have been much harder to adapt to than lockdown in the quiet, book-lined studies of their middle-aged colleagues.

*"Be aware that software is developing in response to new working arrangements and patterns. Might breakout/networking rooms be used to recreate the relational glue that holds our rough edges together?"*

- Investigate the use of standardised backdrops that do not show off your artwork, but create a level playing field with colleagues (as meeting in the office would have done).
- Do not take anyone or his or her contribution for granted. They have opened up their homes and possibly their families to their colleagues and clients. This must be respected and valued.
- Cherish the benefits of the online environment, such as the levelling of playing fields for legal teams across different locations – whether that is across the United Kingdom or around the globe. It really does not matter where your team is; the old hierarchies (eg, London v Rest of the UK/World) no longer apply. Some global teams have thrived in the equality of location. When lockdown is eased and some or all of us can work from places of our choosing, think about maintaining online meetings so as not to revert to an 'us/them' environment that marginalises those working 'away from the office' (even THE office).

Our communities need trust in the same way they need oxygen. Be ambitious and authentic; care and be creative; be connected and committed. You may be surprised by what then happens.

# V. Partners will foot the bill

### 1. Yes – but maybe not straight away

It is well known that law firm partners are both the first into a recession and the first out of one. This homespun truth is a consequence of the profit sharing that is an essential characteristic of being a partner[25] in any firm. At a most basic level, profit is the last element of a firm's financial performance, in the sense that it is what remains once overheads have been covered. In times of 'boom', it is more; in times of 'bust', it is less. Or perhaps more accurately for legal teams, it is more in times of boom *and* bust; it is times of stagnation and stasis that are more difficult:

- Legal teams thrive on change – whether that is born of economic bears or bulls. Buying and selling produce transactional work and a proportion of disputes; regulation continues to produce risk that needs to be understood, quantified and managed. As the song goes, "It all makes work for the working ['*lawyer*'] to do".[26]
- For the same reasons, uncertainty and nervousness for the future limit change. Cash is king and it's usually better to hold on to what you have than to buy or sell; as regards regulatory change, adaptation is contemplated only if it is absolutely necessary, and then with as few bells and whistles as possible (and for this purpose, lawyers might fall into the 'bells and whistles' category).

As we have identified, 16 March 2020 was the day on which the United Kingdom changed as we entered the first lockdown. The truth is that by then, there had already been a slowdown in activity for some time due to a number of factors, including:

- the uncertainty surrounding Brexit terms;
- a growing realisation of law firms' vulnerability to cyberattack; and
- the increased appetite of US firms for London lawyers and the consequent salary war.

However, unlike previous economic crises (most recently, the global financial crisis of 2008/9), the COVID-19 crisis affected everyone. Initially, that effect was operational – as opposed to, for example, the banks realising their exposure to sub-prime lending in the United States and the consequential impact on their ability to finance the economy. The operational crisis ushered in by the COVID-19 pandemic affected the ability of all businesses (including legal teams) to operate, resulting in economic damage and hardship.

Elsewhere, with business revenue on hold, the clients of legal teams had to make cuts to non-essential outgoings while they adjusted their operations and thus their operational staff. Change: good for lawyers.

*"Like many impacts of the pandemic (so far), the emerging financial picture is more of the acceleration of existing trends, rather than new and radical changes."*

At a strategic level, one imagines that the financial models and facilities of businesses also came under review, renegotiation and re-documentation. More change: good for lawyers.

In some particularly hard-hit sectors, where operational and financial change was not viable and thus impossible, there was a spate of insolvencies. Change (drastic change): good for lawyers.

It was therefore somewhat predictable that the last two months of most law firms' 2019/20 financial years were not as significantly affected as might have been feared. The trends were down, but not perhaps as much as one might have equated with a global event on the scale of the pandemic. PwC reported as follows:[27]

> *Whilst the financial performance of UK law firms has been impacted by COVID-19, further analysis underlines the fact that there was ongoing economic pressure in the legal sector prior to the pandemic. Our findings this year suggest that pressure on profitability exists more now than ever, with 42% of Top 100 firms reporting a fall in profits. This is up from 36% in 2019 and 30% in 2018.*
>
> *Whilst 70% of Top 100 law firms reported fee income growth this year, this is notably down on prior years (from 89% in 2019 and 84% in 2018), and absolute growth levels have reduced.*
>
> *The Top 10 trend of falling net profit margins continues into its sixth year and this year's fall is significant, from 35.5% to 33.8% (this is 6.2 percentage points below the 40% high in 2014).*

Like many impacts of the pandemic (so far), the emerging financial picture is more of an acceleration of existing trends, rather than new and radical changes. This is important when we consider the ability of legal teams to 'bounce back' in 2021 and beyond – see later.

**2. Survival of the fittest?**

What's more, the better-managed firms and teams had learned from their experience of the 2008/9 global financial crisis how to navigate through very significant financial adjustments (and how not to!). For partners, deferred value added tax payments, suspended profit distributions and reduced drawings (payments made on account of profits) all contributed to short-term relief. For staff, reduced working weeks in transactional departments, minimum levels of leave to be taken over the summer, good management of financial exposures and the value tied up in working capital and credit control were deployed efficiently and without too much fuss, to buy time to adjust to the COVID-19 world. Added to which, this time round the government offered help in the form of furlough payments (utilised for lawyers and support teams) and loans – so there was less of the drama and mass redundancies of 2008/9.

More sophisticated technical capabilities and the flexibility to work remotely also proved crucial. If lawyers simply worked the time they used to spend commuting, the overall impact on profitability would be immaterial.[28]

Interestingly, and perhaps unsurprisingly, the larger firms' flexible working/resourcing businesses had a good year. Pinsent Masons' Vario expanded into Germany (having previously operated in the United Kingdom and Asia-Pacific); in November 2020, Keystone Law reported that 16 new partners had joined during the pandemic; and Eversheds Sutherlands partners enjoyed an early Christmas, selling the company secretarial arm of their Konexo UK business for a reported £20 million in cash to Law Debenture (representing a c9.0 private equity ratio).[29]

These successes cannot be attributed to COVID-19; after all, 16 March was in week 46 of the financial year to 30 April 2020. The possible exception might reflect the inherent value of an established business with a strong future. As discussed, agile working came of age during the first lockdown and will not look back. Perhaps the development of the legal resourcing market is evidence of this.

However, the same cannot be said of all legal teams. It might have been possible to make some salary savings, but for many teams, overheads are fixed and cannot be adjusted (eg, indemnity premiums, IT costs, unmetered utilities); while those that can be adjusted (eg, sometimes rent) require agreement. Of course, savings were made in front-of-house and catering services; client entertaining and travel vanished overnight, and the connected roles were rendered redundant in the true sense of the term (ie, they ceased to exist). But for many, the 2019/20 financial year was a difficult one, with the pandemic exacerbating existing and worrying trends.

### 3. What's next?

As we look to the future, the key question is whether this is merely a blip and whether, alongside mass vaccination in 2021, we will see a return if not to the record levels of some performance metrics of 2019,[30] then at least to the historic projections for performance in 2020/21.

Back to PwC, whose survey of many UK law firms provides cause for mild optimism, with all sub-sectors of the Top 100 UK law firms[31] predicting improved profitability – in many cases, of a level to make good the adverse movement of 2020. Table 2 sets out the law firms' experience and predictions, as of June 2020.[32]

**Table 2. A predicted bounce-back?**

| Sub-sector of the Top 100 | 2020 % (adverse) movement | 2021 % positive movement | Net % position discounting compound growth |
|---|---|---|---|
| 1–10 | (6.5) | 3.3 | (3.2) |
| 11–25 | (10.2) | 9.4 | (0.8) |
| 26–50 | (20.5) | 21.5 | 1.0 |
| 51–100 | (18.2) | 16.8 | (1.4) |

So it seems that law firms are predicting (or at least hoping for) a blip – a lost year's profitability that is not recovered, but is at least realised in 2021/22 to within 1.5%, apart from in the Magic Circle. The reasons for this pessimism are matters of conjecture at this point in time; look out for our second edition (!).[33]

But more generally, we might not be so convinced by the Top 100's optimism. As noted, the pandemic might be said to have exacerbated existing trends across the financial performance of the UK Top 100. This might also be a reason for the Magic Circle's relative pessimism (or perhaps realism).

Here are some thoughts as to why:

- Virtually all legal teams will have suffered financially as a result of the pandemic. When the impact of Brexit is taken into account, legal teams can expect severe downward pressure on their charges. Lawyers have long been regarded as expensive and their obsession with the hourly rate (shared, albeit with some reluctance, by many in-house teams) means that they wear their financial hearts on their sleeves.
- While transparency is to be applauded, one wonders whether the pandemic and the ensuing austerity will bring about the long-overdue death of the hourly rate as the primary means of valuing lawyers' work and setting their charges, once and for all. If it is not the cause of such a revolution, it may nevertheless be the occasion. As firms and teams develop client/user-acceptable applications and artificial intelligence (AI) solutions to legal problems and services that can execute in a fraction of the time that it took teams of lawyers, firms will be keen to move away from the hourly rate, which implicitly regards every lawyer's

work as artisan craft. This shift will necessitate a recalibration of lawyers' charges. It may be that 'bet the farm' business will continue to be paid for on the basis of time and materials, but 'business as usual' will be unable to survive (or perhaps, this fate will beset the firms that seek to continue with 'business as usual').

- Even the legal profession (or at least, those most in touch with clients/the real world) is struggling with the notion of paying newly qualified solicitors a six-figure salary[34] on the basis of value for money. There are examples of such lawyers being paid salaries that have overtaken those of 'top-end' investment bankers and accountants. In particular, the world's largest law firm, Chicago-based Kirkland & Ellis, is said to be paying more than £140,000 to junior lawyers on qualification.[35] There has subsequently been some retreat from this high-water mark. However, this may be temporary.
- If or when newly qualified lawyers are again offered more than £100,000 by Magic Circle and US firms, we might expect the same reflections that "This cannot be right" when many clients pay a lot less to their equivalent and most promising talent (some with PhDs and post-doctoral experience). This might be even more the case on the other side of the pandemic, when the perceived value and rewards of scientific qualifications stand to be celebrated. In short, the current financial model of UK law firms is overdue a recalibration.[36]
- In response to COVID-19, many law firms have taken action around their external financing. The Top 50 UK law firms, taken as a whole, increased their external finance as a larger proportion of overall funding, with the most significant increases in the Top 11–25, up from 21% to 28%; and in the Top 26–50, up from 12% to 17%. The increased cost of finance, if not paid off promptly, will become a fixed cost for law firms that they will be unable to pass on to clients – possibly at all and not, one expects, to an extent that would facilitate the bounce-back in profitability that is predicted. The relative increases in external funding are material: 29% for the Top 26–50 and 42% for the Top 51–100.[37]
- Further, the COVID-19 pandemic has elevated the priority of working capital management to an absolute necessity and hence we have seen further improvement in firms' year-end 'lock-up performance'[38]. All sub-sectors of the UK's Top 100 firms improved, with the Top 51–100 firms making the most substantial reductions (for the fourth consecutive year), from 133 days to 119 days.[39] Therefore, there is less cash-flow value in reserve – good for retiring partners; less so, perhaps, for those who are continuing (and joining the partnership) – and less cash-flow value for a rainy day/year.

*"The COVID-19 pandemic has elevated the priority of working capital management to an absolute necessity and hence we have seen further improvement in firms' year-end 'lock-up performance'."*

Cost savings are therefore set to be a feature of the next few years for all legal teams, unless partners realign their expectations. We do not discount the prospect of such a realignment. Lifestyle changes brought about by the pandemic might have become treasured, especially by those senior lawyers who lost their private space at the office and have rediscovered it in lockdown; likewise, peace and quiet in which to work and think. The prospect of commuting to open-plan workspaces after what looks to be more than a year away might for some balance the books against reduced profitability (which in any event might be mitigated by a revised real estate strategy).

**4. Think the unthinkable**

We want to encourage lawyers – whether in firms, in businesses or in teams – and their clients to think the unimaginable and plan to deliver. Surely, it would have been unthinkable in 2019 that lawyers would be forced to dislocate and relocate away from working habits that have largely remained unchanged for decades; and yet here we are, not having been to our office-based desks, at the time of writing, for more than a year. We have done the unthinkable once – so why not again? Here are some thoughts on what might come into view in the near future for legal teams to build on, rather than retreat from, the COVID-19 response – which some might say has brought out the best in (the best) legal teams:

- Clients have suffered too – listen to their concerns and do so initially with empty notepads and insightful questions. Recycle other clients' experiences (anonymously).
- Rethink your real estate strategy and remember it is not a one size fits all (it never was, but maybe that is acknowledged now – and once that genie is out of the bottle...).
- Develop a talent attraction strategy that is not dependent on salary, whether alone or in the main. Those motivated by more and more money are unlikely to be long-term bets anyway. Let them and their egos affect (infect) another team.
- Use AI to better allocate work and to overcome unconscious bias that delegates on line of sight.
- Use AI in support functions to deliver efficiencies at levels of cost and profitability that are recognised as valuable and sustainable.
- Develop and promote a charging/working philosophy that promotes your people's wellbeing (and remember, it's not easy to become, let alone continue life as, a work-shy lawyer) and client respect (loyalty will deepen).
- Recognise – actively – that agile and remote working is here to stay and invest in your people's successful adoption of it, especially those who care for children and/or work part time.

*"Report on more than law firm and partner profitability. What is the legal team equivalent to the triple bottom line that paints a more holistic picture of what you do?"*

- Report on more than law firm and partner profitability. What is the legal team equivalent to the triple bottom line that paints a more holistic picture of what you do? Embrace it and who knows, maybe the *Legal 500* and other measurers will follow suit.
- As the technological demands increase, recognise that some of your people might be left behind. Find new ways to engage their talents for the benefit of your stakeholders and/or develop new ways of moving towards retirement. In its law firm survey, PwC noted rising levels of capacity, especially at the senior grades within law firms; and the same must be true of legal teams.[40] As we now have a better appreciation of wellbeing, what insights beyond corporate memory (itself of high value, especially for those who have led and worked through the pandemic's dislocation and relocation) can be shared and respected?
- What audacious plans for the development and benefit of your legal team and its stakeholder beneficiaries have been on the back burner for some time and/or consigned to the 'too difficult' list that could ride the wave of successful adaptation? Get them out there before we slide (or even race) back to normal. Note also the implications for your external, if not internal, stakeholders of going back... Is that *really* what you want to do/be known for?

These ideas, and countless others like them, may not deliver immediate financial returns; but they will improve the quality of your offering and attract value across your stakeholder beneficiary community. And where there's value, there's an economy – and one you can shape.

# VI. A changed profession: will old values still triumph?

## 1. Keep calm and carry on lawyering?

In many ways, one of the qualities that clients most appreciate in a legal team is the ability not to panic – to keep calm and carry on. The objectivity and lack of emotion for which lawyers are famous were at a premium in the first days of dislocation. During the first lockdown (March to July 2020), when there was a sense that the pandemic was a short-term disruption, the lawyerly mindset effectively declared that if we kept our heads and kept on lawyering, we would soon be back to normal.

Our hardwired association of September with new beginnings was apt. Against this backdrop, it was more than tempting to seek comfort in the time-honoured qualities of lawyers (analytical skills, sound judgement, interpersonal skills, good communications and perseverance),[41] and believe that they would see legal teams – and indeed, the profession – through to the other side of the pandemic and into the sunlit uplands of a post-COVID-19, post-Brexit world. We would soon be back in the office and operating as we used to.

These skills have stood, and will continue to stand, legal teams in good stead. We have already commented on the importance of many of them – in particular, good communication and people skills. We are not saying that these necessarily come naturally to lawyers or that they have been developed further during the pandemic; it seems more that the pandemic has revealed, rather than shaped, the better legal team leaders and managers. But it must be right (mustn't it?) that if we continue to hone these skills and enhance our professionalism – the essential qualities of trust and discretion -- then the legal team toolkit should be complete for the short term and might also survive the temporary immersion into an online era.

However, the dislocation from the office was so severe that maintaining the status quo became increasingly difficult; increasingly unlikely. This is not to say that legal teams had many other ideas or plans. The talk was still of the 'new normal'. We had worked through the dislocation (well, sort of) and the transition was beginning to yield dividends (save perhaps for those on whom the burden of 'home schooling' fell). Agile legal teams were just that, only for longer. 'Same-dom' ("What day is it again?") and isolation became the enemies, rather than the dislocation *per se* (so long as we remembered to unmute).

But as time has passed, the absence of precedent (a word that is music to lawyers' ears and the absence of which is something of a challenge) began to characterise the situation that legal teams found themselves in: they had no point of reference. While it is natural to seek solace in the familiar structures and approaches of the past, as we have struggled through Lockdowns 2 and 3, there seems to have emerged an accompanying sense of the need (or perhaps more accurately, the opportunity) for change.

The question then is whether legal teams – and more pointedly, lawyers – can make the changes that their stakeholders are asking for or might be open to. Experience might tell us that it is difficult enough acting for or advising entrepreneurs, let alone emulating them. Indeed, there are plenty who say (or even hope) that lawyers and legal teams won't have to change, as change never comes alone; it arrives as a result of equally unfamiliar activities such as imagination, innovation and collaboration. Some have put it more starkly:

> *Lawyers and entrepreneurs make strange bedfellows. Lawyers look 'backwards' at precedents while entrepreneurs look 'forward' to the launch of a new business or new product. Lawyers are generally conservative and risk-averse while their clients are optimistic and willing to take chances to achieve their goals.*[42]

This is not to say that all lawyers are trapped by precedent or *stare decisis*. Transactional lawyers might believe that they have been weaned off such inclinations. However, this is undeniably how lawyers are taught and rewarded for their learning; and what their clients have valued in the past as features of robust, reliable legal analysis.[43] So the chances are that this mindset runs deep. The 'chicken and egg' debate applies: are lawyers trained to be like this or do those with the appropriate mindset gravitate towards law school? That is for another time; for current purposes, it doesn't matter. What matters is how these "left-brained: logical, analytical and objective" people and teams can avail of these opportunities for innovation and development which are usually the preserve of the "right brained: intuitive, thoughtful and subjective".[44]

## 2. Or might fortune favour the brave?

*Brave?!*[45] If not brave, then perhaps *humble*?

Some context: it was Tim Zagat – a corporate lawyer who gave up practice in the late 1970s to found the "world's original provider of user-generated content", in the form of a restaurant guide – who said, "Anyone who is intelligent enough and has worked hard enough to become a lawyer can become a success in a myriad of fields."[46] True, possibly; flattering, probably – but in fact, something of a barrier to effective innovation when we know, or perhaps have read and/or observed in our clients, that collaboration and even dissonance are the key ingredients for innovation and change.

The insightful Professor Michele DeStefano[47] is a leading proponent of innovation for lawyers. In *New Suits: Appetite for Disruption in the Legal World*,[48] which explores the need and opportunity for lawyers to disrupt, she observes that without an understanding of both the lawyer's identity as a legal professional and the lawyer as an individual (each of which is ingrained as a result of education and experience), "our efforts at innovation will be stymied".[49] Further, lawyers "don't want to be entrepreneurs. At most, they may want to be intrapreneurs":[50] those who have the qualities and skills of an entrepreneur, but who seek to promote innovation internally, within the organisation, company or firm (or legal team) in which they work.

If DeStefano is right, there may be few brave lawyers whom fortune might favour. But there are two key questions for the post-COVID-19 legal team to grapple with:

- Will it be acceptable to clients and colleague for legal teams to revert to pre-March 2020 ways of working (for which, read also billing and so on)? And if this was an acceptable position to adopt following the first lockdown, then what about after the second and third lockdowns?
- If not, will it be possible for law teams to change from the old ways of doing and being, even if they want to?

*"While legal teams have been* operationally *adaptable,* constitutionally *they are still liable to lazy thinking about measures of success, criteria for promotion and so on."*

Surveying the situation after 12 months of lockdown, the signs suggest that teams are both more adaptable than might have been thought before the pandemic (and we might be surprised at who has adapted), and more conservative/traditional about their core values. So while legal teams have been *operationally* adaptable, *constitutionally* they are still liable to lazy thinking about measures of success, criteria for promotion and so on. This chimes with DeStefano's analysis: we have been able to adapt *how* we operate, but most of us have lacked the necessary capacity (or time) to reimagine *what* we do.

We would therefore suggest that if legal teams seek to return to the pre-March 2020 environment, they will have missed an opportunity to plan and implement a more dramatic and strategic exit from the challenges of the pandemic. Indeed, the language of 'return' speaks for itself.

At this juncture, let us not overlook how some of the institutions of law have adapted to operating in the COVID-19 world. The courts in particular had committed to online dispute resolution for many years, and Money Claims Online (through which court proceedings can be issued online without having to deliver documents to the court office, with all the perils that involves) has been operating since 2001, with 180,000 users annually.[51] More recent information is available through a specialist website: Remote Courts Worldwide[52] records how justice systems have responded to the challenges of online hearings.

A report from the Honourable Justice Eniola A Fabamwo of the Nigerian High Court is particularly encouraging evidence of a rethink of normal but outdated practices for online times:

> *Preliminary applications and mentions, sometimes which consist of only one sentence by the lawyer such as "we will like to schedule the case for trial" or "we will like to serve the party by substituted means" ought to be heard remotely without the inconvenience of long hours of travel and long hours of queuing in stuffy court halls…*
>
> *[We operate a] hybrid situation whereby complex or suitable cases for trial involving a lot of exhibits are heard in 'open court' and applications are heard remotely or online will benefit ALL post-covid19 or post-pandemic times.*
>
> *Practice Direction No 2 signed by the Chief Judge of Ogun State in May 2020, where I preside, has enabled me to experiment with this hybrid court. As at today, I have had no less than 100 remote sittings which have involved not only applications but full trials at the request of the parties and this experience has been most rewarding to all as it saves time and cost.*[53]

The UK courts have risen to the challenge by way of a new practice direction which was informed by a state of mind described here by Sir Geoffrey Vos, the then chancellor of the High Court, having heard an appeal in *Teesside Gas Transportation Ltd v Cats North Sea Ltd*:[54]

> *I want only to mention briefly the way in which the hearing of this appeal was conducted. Thanks to the hard work and cooperation of court staff, the parties and their lawyers, this appeal was conducted entirely remotely by the use of Skype for Business. It was completed comfortably within the 1.5-day estimate, and both leading counsel had a proper opportunity to make their submissions, to confer with their junior counsel, and to take proper instructions from their instructing solicitors and clients. It was obviously not possible during the current coronavirus pandemic for the hearing safely to be conducted in court whilst observing the necessary social distancing. Some 19 individuals, including the members of the court, were signed in to the Skype conferencing facility at any one time. …*
>
> *I have explained how this hearing was undertaken in an attempt to demonstrate the flexibility of the arrangements that can be made, with the cooperation of the parties and their lawyers, to continue*

> *to deliver fair, open and transparent justice in a period of national difficulty.*

Looking at the announcements of UK law firms during the pandemic, we can see that projects that may have started before March 2020 have been pushed through to completion in the areas of international expansion[55] and innovation;[56] and individual lawyers have seen for themselves the benefits of different ways of working and organising themselves.[57]

The signs are that many law teams are embracing the opportunities from enforced lockdown – capitalising on, and perhaps measuring, the benefits of this dislocation (eg, tonnes of carbon saved from not commuting and reduced air travel). We can expect changes in real estate strategy to follow when leases and so on permit.

But what about the more difficult stuff? Law teams emerging from the pandemic have the opportunity to renew and evidence their commitment to:

- promoting diversity and inclusion;
- delivering and advising on environmental change;
- adopting practices – including pricing – that drive appropriate/client-centred service; and
- promoting a location-centric culture for firms, teams and courts.[58]

Whether lawyers, or a sufficient number of them, have the capacity to make lasting and insightful change for the better remains to be seen; but there are signs of hope in what might have been thought of as unexpected places.

### 3. "Brave? Me?!"

In his latest work *Think Again*,[59] Wharton Business School organisational psychologist Professor Adam Grant urges us to explore how rethinking happens. He suggests that we need to spend more time considering how we change our minds, how we persuade others and how we build cultures of lifelong learning. The pandemic in the truest sense has been an invitation for all of us to let go of knowledge and opinions that no longer serve us well. In Grant's eyes, flexibility is more desirable than consistency. This view, of course, does not acquit itself well in the legal profession, with its emphasis on *stare decisis*. Lawyers by nature love consistency – often at the expense of flexibility. We follow previously decided cases that put up similar facts and issues. When transactional lawyers sit down to negotiate a new deal, they look to previous transactions to see which points they conceded to the other side last time round and which points they fought like cats and dogs to keep. Precedent, for lawyers, is the certainty and consistency we crave in legal practice and in our professional lives.

What does it mean for a lawyer to be more flexible? Before we get to that, let's first explore the concept of 'flexible lawyers'. The idea of 'flexible lawyering' – that lawyers can jump in and out of employment engagements, balancing their other obligations and commitments just as the organisations that hire them do, based on their needs and workflow – is not what we are talking about here.

When we talk about lawyers being more flexible, we mean having a presence of mind that does not automatically presume to know what should happen today, tomorrow or the day after that. This, of course, goes against our expectations of lawyers, in that they are usually the go-to planners for all contingencies, real and imagined. Presence of mind is that state of awareness in which we are focused exclusively on the task in front of us, wholly and with all our attention, as opposed to wandering off distractedly in a myriad of multi-tasking directions. The antithesis is that moment when your mind stops wandering as you are driving down the M1 and you realise that you have not been paying the slightest bit of attention to what is going on in front of you on the highway.

*"Precedent, for lawyers, is the certainty and consistency we crave in legal practice and in our professional lives."*

Knowing directly what is going on both inside and outside ourselves, from moment to moment, is the mindfulness that we need to be flexible lawyers. According to Professor Mark Williams, formerly of the Oxford Mindfulness Centre: "It's easy to stop noticing the world around us. It's also easy to lose touch with the way our bodies are feeling and to end up living 'in our heads' – caught up in our thoughts without stopping to notice how those thoughts are driving our emotions and behaviour."[60]

### 4. Flexible lawyers – great lawyers

So why do we say here, "Brave? Me!"? Perhaps we can use the pandemic to rethink where the legal profession should be headed – not in grand terms, but at an individual level. This is not to advocate a grand rethink of who we are and how we operate as lawyers. What we are talking about is rather redefining the qualities of a great lawyer or a great legal team, and engaging with the possibilities of the future. The qualities that will be needed to do so include the following:

- Empathy: Getting serious about seeing the world through other eyes and hunting down other perspectives. The teams that do this could unleash unimaginable dynamism.
- Imagination: Not being so wedded to the past or to precedent,

*"Perhaps we can use the pandemic to rethink where the legal profession should be headed – not in grand terms, but at an individual level."*

and remembering that the law is a fast-changing phenomenon (so why do lawyers fear change?).

- Innovation: This follows imagination.
- Courage: Because it is easy not to be courageous, and we can be risk averse beyond what is helpful.
- Honesty: Just because the status quo could be worse, doesn't mean we have to live with it.
- Social change (justice, even?): Can we use our skills to make the world a fairer, better place than we found it before COVID-19?
- Using existing strategies and vehicles where possible, but not being afraid to make new starts: because there is no point reinventing the wheel.

### 4.1 Empathy

The American Psychological Association defines 'empathy' as "understanding a person from his or her frame of reference rather than one's own, or vicariously experiencing that person's feelings, perceptions, and thoughts".[61] The same definition "does not, of itself, entail motivation to be of assistance";[62] it may turn into sympathy or personal distress, which may result in action. Section 3.4 of the Bar Standards Board's Professional Statement for Barristers (2016) refers to the need to know how and when to demonstrate empathy.[63] Noted psychologist Daniel Goleman characterises the dilemma that lawyers face on this point rather exquisitely: "We often emphasize the importance of keeping cool in a crisis. But sometimes coolness can give way to detachment and apathy."[64] So what is the right balance to strike here? Goleman points to his colleague Paul Ekman, who suggests that the right kind of empathy is "compassionate empathy", whereby we not only understand a person's predicament and feel with them, but are spontaneously moved to help if needed: "[S]ometimes we must let ourselves get hot to help."[65]

For a good example of empathy, we can look to fictional lawyer Atticus Finch from Harper Lee's *To Kill A Mockingbird*:[66]

> *He understands the importance of empathy. After Scout complains about her teacher's draconian perspective on reading, Atticus consoles her by offering wisdom about a better way to deal with people: "If you can learn a simple trick, Scout, you'll get along a lot better with all kinds of folks. You never really understand a person until you consider things from his point of view — until you climb into his skin and walk around in it."*[67]

Admittedly, most of us will never achieve the same level of empathy as Finch; and today it is also hotly contested whether he deserves to be called a hero[68] when considered in a contemporary light. But nonetheless, Finch's simple encomium of empathy from the pages of literature still rings true today.

## 4.2 Imagination

As we dig deeper into the concept of the flexible lawyer, further reflection on the theme of imagination is needed. *Law and Imagination in Troubled Times: A Legal and Literary Discourse*[69] eloquently makes the case for imagination in legal practice:

> *There is no doubt that imagination in general, and legal imagination, is of the utmost importance... it is also useful when it comes to reshaping legal norms in response to novel circumstances. It is something ... that every lawyer, judge and legal scholar who thinks seriously about their practice should strive to acquire.*

But how is imagination nurtured when it clashes with legal reality? Here we can look to the words of Albert Einstein, who wrote that:

> *[I]magination is more important than knowledge. For knowledge is limited, whereas imagination embraces the entire world, stimulating progress, giving birth to evolution. It is, strictly speaking, a real factor in scientific research.*[70]

Creative thinking in law is essential; but to be honest, not all of us are Albert Einstein.

## 4.3 Creativity

In writing on how in-lawyers can become more creative, Turner and Krantz suggest starting small:

> *Creative thinking involves the generation and implementation of ideas that are both novel and useful. While 'big C' Creativity involves ground-breaking ideas that are novel to the world, 'little c' creativity includes coming up with new solutions to everyday problems.*[71]

In distinguishing between convergent and divergent thinking, Turner and Frantz urge us to harness both types of thought. Divergent thinking typically involves developing a list of options or ways to accomplish a particular task; while convergent thinking involves evaluating, prioritising, synthesising or selecting from among different options in a systematic and disciplined fashion after carefully weighing the options.[72] By working with both alternative approaches, you can select the best options that are viable, yet still break new ground to bring creativity to bear on problems big and small in the workplace.

## 4.4 Innovation

We also mention the importance of innovation. First, however, we must distinguish between creativity and innovation, and explain how they differ. Creativity is the act of conceiving something new; while innovation is the act of putting that concept into practice. Reena Sengupta – the owner of RSG Consulting and founder of the FT Innovative Lawyer series of reports and awards – cautions against confusing innovation with invention:

> *You don't have to invent the next legal iPod®; innovation is about improvement. Its constantly saying: How can I do better for our clients? How can I run our team better? How can we deliver legal advice better?*[73]

Sengupta readily admits that lawyers may be disinclined towards innovation, in that the 'archetypal lawyer' tends to be more risk averse and detail focused, trained to look for mistakes and less forgiving of experimentation or tolerant of failure. So what distinguishes an innovative lawyer? Sengupta says that innovators are both incredibly analytical and bold and willing to try new things and take risks. They see the big picture and the even bigger picture; they spot the problems in front of them on the road and those beyond the bend that no one else can see.[74]

One example of how a risk-averse mentality can impede development of the law can be found in the US law on the sale of goods. The United

*"Lawyers may be disinclined towards innovation, in that the 'archetypal lawyer' tends to be more risk averse and detail focused, trained to look for mistakes and less forgiving of experimentation or tolerant of failure."*

States has ratified the United Nations Convention on Contracts for the International Sale of Goods (CISG), which came into effect under federal law on 1 January 1988. However, US commercial lawyers were unfamiliar with the CISG and how it operated in conjunction with state law. As a result, they universally recommended that their clients not incorporate the CISG into contracts with individuals in other CISG contracting states. This led to the slow adoption of the CISG in the United States, the loss of about 20 years of US case law interpreting the provisions of the CISG and the inability of US commercial clients to take advantage of some of the more flexible provisions of the CISG when compared to the state law Uniform Commercial Code (UCC) provisions that most lawyers felt more comfortable using. And this lack of innovative thinking is not limited to one side of the Atlantic: remarkably, the United Kingdom remains the only major trading nation not to have adopted the CISG into its domestic law, preferring instead to use its own arcane equivalent to the UCC, the Sale of Goods Act 1979.

## 4.5 Courage

We recognise courage as a trait that lawyers should demonstrate, especially in the age of COVID-19 and in the new world we will face once the pandemic is over. Courage is easy to spot, but impossible to define. What makes for a courageous lawyer in current times? What should we do when, for instance, the media and politicians attack members of the Bar, solicitors and even judges? Prime Minister Boris Johnson attacked "lefty human rights lawyers" in a Conservative conference speech in October 2020.[75] Home Secretary Priti Patel went even further and "grouped 'the do-gooders, the lefty lawyers, the Labour Party' with 'the traffickers' in her claim that people giving 'grand lectures on human rights' and saying they were 'defending the indefensible'".[76] Can lawyers sit back and do nothing while their colleagues are attacked for carrying out their duty to apply the law irrespective of political persuasion or the popularity of those they represent?

And it is not only attacks from our political leaders that we must worry about. The media has also launched savage invectives against judges for their decisions, in what constitutes a clear risk to the principle of an independent judiciary. For example, on 4 November 2016 James Slack – the former political editor at the *Daily Mail* and later Prime Minister Theresa May's official spokesperson – wrote an article about three judges who had ruled that the UK government required the consent of Parliament to give notice of Brexit. Slack's headline (which was approved by then editor Paul Dacre), which was emblazoned across the front page of the *Daily Mail*, called them out as "ENEMIES OF THE PEOPLE".[77] Beneath the pictures of the judges, bewigged and robed in all their judicial finery, was the strapline: "Fury of 'out of

*"Can lawyers sit back and do nothing while their colleagues are attacked for carrying out their duty to apply the law irrespective of political persuasion or the popularity of those they represent?"*

touch' judges who defied 17.4 m Brexit voters and could trigger constitutional crisis." The article went on to attack the three senior members of the judiciary – Lord Chief Justice Lord Thomas, Lord Justice Sales and Sir Terence Etherton. Its attack on the latter was particularly personal, describing the master of the rolls as an "openly-gay ex-Olympic fencer". However, this abuse by the *Daily Mail* had absolutely no effect on the willingness of these judges, or other members of the judiciary, to make tough decisions on Brexit without fear or intimidation. The individual courage that the judges demonstrated in the face of such invective was an inspirational demonstration of judicial independence; they proved themselves 'profiles in courage' that should inspire the entire profession.

### 4.6 Make COVID-19 a manifesto for change in society

We will have to be honest with ourselves and accept that certain situations that existed before COVID-19 are no longer acceptable post-pandemic. COVID-19 made winners and losers of different organisations and aspects of life. First, the pandemic hit women in the workplace far harder than men: "When women have to juggle their corporate day jobs along with a disproportionate share of family caregiving and housekeeping the situation gets grim fast. Study after study tells the tale."[78] So what will leaders in the legal profession do to address this problem, because the status quo is no longer good enough?

Second, up to 1.3 million overseas nationals have left the United Kingdom since January 2020, with almost 700,000 foreign-born workers having vacated London alone, according to one study.[79] It is clear that, faced with the twin prospects of no job or reduced pay and the high cost of accommodation, many European workers in service industry roles chose to return home to their families to escape both the health and financial threats of COVID-19. What does this say about the ease with which we took it for granted, pre-COVID-19, that someone would always be around to serve us coffee in the morning; to take us home in the small hours after a night on the town; to empty our wastepaper baskets and vacuum the floors at our offices? Even worse, what does it say about us as a society that we see a whole class of people who perform thankless tasks for low wages as expendable; and that their departure does not even ring alarm bells about social inequality and invisibility because they are foreign born?

Third, we have failed the young. New entrants to the legal profession have lost two recruitment seasons. The annual routine of bringing on new university graduates and trainees to join legal teams has been disrupted twice. The first thing to go when the pandemic started was the hiring of new talent. Everyone put a freeze on hiring and, even worse, cancelled recruitment programmes, work placements and

*"Through issues such as 'vaccine nationalism', COVID-19 has laid bare the widening gap between the 'haves' and the 'have nots'. The pandemic has heightened the pre-existing cracks in our global world order."*

similar initiatives. What can we do to make this up to the new talent out there? Has the legal profession lost many of these gifted university graduates and trainees? What will we do once things pick up again? Will we have all the talent we need when demand returns?

Finally, even if our legal teams may have survived the pandemic, health-wise and otherwise, many of our clients and business partners will have lost everything. Many of the businesses that were our partners in the past have vanished. Certain businesses may never recover from the pandemic. Greater efforts must be made to understand the trauma of lost dreams and to help people to recover and rebuild the dignity lost when the pandemic destroyed their businesses, livelihoods and dreams. In October 2020, Culture Secretary Oliver Dowden pulled a cringeworthy government ad that encouraged people who worked in the arts to retrain.[80] The ad – which featured an image of a ballerina with the strapline, "Fatima's next job could be in cyber (she just doesn't know it yet)" – was criticised as crass by Dowden; but it highlighted the perception that the government does not value the arts as highly as other industries it sees as more essential to society.

Social change is needed now more than ever. Through issues such as 'vaccine nationalism', COVID-19 has laid bare the widening gap between the 'haves' and the 'have nots'. The pandemic has heightened the pre-existing cracks in our global world order. We need to address these as a society and as a profession, because there will come a point at which both our society and the legal profession will be unable to shield themselves from the consequences of a global world order in which so few have so much, while most make do with very little. If we think that we will be safe in our advanced societies, with wealth and access to vaccines, while poverty and disease rage elsewhere, we are fooling ourselves. If the wealth and health gaps between nations are not addressed, global unrest will follow. It is obscene to see billionaires fight like children in the playground to spend millions to become the first tourists in space when 690 million humans go to bed every night hungry. The fact that a 20-year-old waiter from New York is likely to get a COVID-19 vaccine before the doctor in Malawi who runs the country's only COVID-19 treatment facility is wrong. Simply put, we cannot go back to the old normal.

### 4.7 Social justice (warriors?)

The social justice agenda is never far from the legal profession. Lawyers have a duty to protect the rights of their clients, promote the cause of justice and work to uphold human rights and fundamental freedoms, while acting freely and diligently in accordance with the law and the recognised standards and ethics of the legal profession.[81] Whether we admit it or not, every lawyer in their own way is a 'social justice warrior' – even if the term has taken on a pejorative sense in the social media age. Katherine Martin, head of US dictionaries at Oxford University Press, is not exactly sure when this switched from being a primarily positive term to an overwhelmingly negative one; she suggests that 2011 appears to have been a turning point, when the insult first appeared on Twitter.[82] Maybe it is about time that lawyers reclaimed the term and flipped it back...

In this discussion, we have made the case for using existing strategies and vehicles, where possible, to fix the shortcomings in legal teams that need addressing, so that we can 'build back better'. While we should not shy away from making new starts, we also recognise that not everything needs to be reinvented. Many things worked well in the legal profession before COVID-19; and to the credit of the profession, the pandemic has shown how resilient it can be when faced with unprecedented challenges. While we should never be afraid to make a new start, there is no need to reinvent the wheel.

### 5. The brakes are coming off – which way now?

The pandemic caused legal teams and their clients to slam on the emergency brakes. So as we get ready to hit the accelerator once again, which direction are we headed in? Surely not the same one, in the same ways, as before? Would that not be odd, given the likely (if not felt) impact of many months of dislocation, isolation and reflection?

When legal scholars examined the effects of the 2008/9 global financial crisis on the legal profession, they reached conclusions that are also applicable today:

> *While some believe that the Great Recession will have permanent adverse effects on the legal profession, it is important to bear in mind that points of significant distress are at the same time moments of great opportunity, and the legal profession, with its track record of adapting to changing practice realities while successfully maintaining its elite professional, financial, and cultural status atop US society may end up stronger than ever ... [T]he possibility of long-term growth, innovation, and resurgence should not be discounted, and claims regarding the death of the profession and some of its leading institutions may be premature.*[83]

The breadth and depth of the COVID-19 pandemic are in some ways more severe than those of the global financial crisis. Yet there is no doubt that the legal profession, and what we call 'Big Law', emerged from the crisis stronger and in many ways with a greater share of the market than before.[84] Much has changed since then, of course: we have seen the emergence of asymmetrical players in the legal field;

the rise of flexible lawyering; and increased use of technology to deliver legal services more efficiently and at a lower cost. Yet while Big Law is stronger than ever, there is also a very solid niche for the asymmetrical players, which continue to thrive as before the pandemic.

If you have the sort of job that allowed you to continue working from home during the pandemic, you are one of the lucky ones. Yes, there were serious obstacles – such as home schooling, self-isolating and caring for shielding parents – that were difficult to handle. However, if demand for your services did not dry up due to COVID-19, you survived. But colleagues with less secure jobs – such as those who depended on agency work for document review or who did court appearance work for others – were not so lucky. Additionally, those who support the legal profession through catering, delivery, office cleaning or taxi services have had a rough time.

## 6. Closing remarks

In this Special Report, we have reflected on a changed profession operating in a changed world. So much has changed since those days in early February 2020 when we looked on with bemusement as a fleet of cranes built temporary hospitals in Wuhan. We marvelled at how mountain goats overtook the town of Llandudno in Wales. We were inspired by Andrea Bocelli singing "Amazing Grace" outside the *Duomo* on Easter Sunday in a deserted Milan. We clapped hard for NHS workers every Thursday night. We were inspired by the Queen's message of hope, "We Will Meet Again". We cheered on Captain Sir Tom Moore as he did laps of his lawn on his walker to raise millions for the NHS. We watched as modern science came to the rescue, providing doctors with a growing armamentarium of treatments and vaccines to fight COVID-19.

The human toll of COVID-19 has been immeasurable. We owe it to the memory of all those we have lost to reimagine a humanity that is far more compassionate and equitable in its treatment of those who are less well off than us. The healthcare professionals and essential workers who selflessly put their lives on the line day after day have been an inspiration to us all. In this pantheon of great sacrifice and noble acts, we in the legal profession can step up our game so that the world we work in after the pandemic is more imaginative, compassionate and supportive of others. If we can do this, we will have come out of COVID-19 better than when we went in. The profession has changed, but the old values endure.

## Notes

1 SRA, "How Diverse is the Legal Profession?", 20 March 2020, www.sra.org.uk/sra/equality-diversity/key-findings/diverse-legal-profession/.
2 M McLuhan and Q Fiore, *The Medium is the Massage: An Inventory of Effects* (Penguin Books, 1967), 123, 126–128.
3 Adam Liptak, "Supreme Court Hears First Arguments via Phone", *New York Times*, 4 May 2020, www.nytimes.com/2020/05/04/us/politics/supreme-court-coronavirus-call.html?searchResultPosition=1.
4 Hannah Wootton, "Lawyers expand, upgrade offices despite remote working push", *Financial Review*, 11 March 2021, www.afr.com/companies/professional-services/lawyers-expand-upgrade-offices-despite-remote-working-push-20210310-p579cp.
5 For which, read also Scottish, Welsh or Northern Irish person, etc.
6 There was a time in the 1990s when mobile phones were for partners only. One of the authors recalls a staff meeting when one of the more rebellious solicitors asked when mobile phones would cease to be a reward for status and properly deployed as a business tool. Answer: in about 20 years.
7 'Fear of missing out'.
8 https://clp.law.harvard.edu/news-post/prof-laura-empson-shines-light-on-insecure-overachievers-on-bbc-radio/.
9 See www.vuca-world.org/.
10 Tom Wall, "Grant Shapps faces fury over mass Covid outbreak at DVLA: Minister under fire for 'shameful' virus spread as staff told to work on with more than 500 cases at agency in Swansea", *The Observer*, 23 January 2021, www.theguardian.com/world/2021/jan/23/minister-faces-fury-over-mass-covid-outbreak-at-top-government-agency.
11 BMA, "COVID-19: Risk assessment", updated as of 18 January 2021, www.bma.org.uk/advice-and-support/covid-19/your-health/covid-19-risk-assessment#:~:text=Current%20evidence%20for%20COVID%2D19,been%20associated%20with%20severe%20disease.
12 For more on the dichotomy between 'work from work' and 'work from home', see the 18 August 2020 *Quest Means Business* television interview of Anthony Malkin, CEO of Empire State Realty Trust, by CNN reporter Zain Asher, www.facebook.com/watch/?v=227798955198019.
13 US Senate Committee on Health, Education Labor & Pensions, "Examining Our COVID-19 Response: An Update from Federal Officials", live replay of testimony of Dr Anthony Fauci, MD, Director, National Institute of Allergy and Infectious Diseases, National Institutes of Health, 18 March 2021, www.help.senate.gov/hearings/examining-our-covid-19-response-an-update-from-federal-officials.
14 Lynsey Addario, "Opinion: It's Still Getting Worse – Inside Britain's Vicious Second Wave", *New York Times*, 28 January 2021, www.nytimes.com/2021/01/28/opinion/uk-covid-deaths-hospitals.html?action=click&module=Opinion&pgtype=Homepage.
15 Robert Galford and Anne Drapeau, "The Enemies of Trust", *Harvard Business Review*, 2003, 81(2), 88–95, 126.
16 Patrick M Lencioni and Kensuke Okabayashi, *The Five Dysfunctions of a Team* (Wiley, 2012), p63 (emphasis added).
17 See DWF's announcement on 10 December 2020, when chief operating officer Matthew Doughty told *City AM:* "Our expectation is that over the next 18 to 24 months we will really start to look at our premises. I think we can shrink the size of our individual premises quite significantly, I think we can occupy them more efficiently by the time we've taken out paper storage; *we can have people coming in and out of the offices a couple of times a week and having people working more remotely"* (emphasis added).
18 Frances X Frei and A Morriss, "Begin With Trust", *HBR Magazine* (May–June 2020), https://hbr.org/2020/05/begin-with-trust.
19 For more about 'check, plan, do', see Vanguard, *Beyond command-and-control*, https://vanguard-method.net/library/systems-principles/check-plan-do/.
20 Malcolm Gladwell, *Blink: The Power of Thinking without Thinking* (Little, Brown and Co, 2005).
21 Kantar, *Purpose 2020 Study – Igniting Purpose Led Growth* (June 2019), https://consulting.kantar.com/wp-content/uploads/2019/06/Purpose-2020-PDF-Presentation.pdf.
22 John Maxwell blog (7 August 2012), www.johnmaxwell.com/blog/are-you-really-leading-or-are-you-just-taking-a-walk/.
23 On 6 October 2007, the New Zealand All Blacks rugby union team crashed out of the Rugby World Cup to France in the quarter-finals. The shock was such that senior members of the squad and team management spent time in retreat to rediscover the essence of an All Black player; this led to the articulation of the qualities and values that they would cherish and live out as a squad. See James Kerr, *Legacy: What the All Blacks Can Teach Us About the Business of Life* (Constable Books, 2013).
24 P Campion and M Langdon, "Achieving multiple topic shifts in primary care medical consultations: a conversation analysis study in UK general practice", *Sociology of Health & Illness*, 2004, 26: 81–101, https://doi.org/10.1111/j.1467-9566.2004.00379.x.
25 That is, an equity or profit-sharing partner.
26 Flanders and Swann, *The Gas Man Cometh* (1964).
27 PwC, *Annual Law Firms' Survey 2020: Embracing Change to Succeed*, www.pwc.co.uk/industries/business-services/law-firms/survey.html.
28 Do the maths.

29 Earnings before interest, tax, depreciation and amortisation estimated to be £2.2 million at the time of sale – see www.stockmarketwire.com/article/7188162/Law-Debenture-acquires-Eversheds-Sutherland-company-secretarial-unit-for-pound20m.html.
30 For example, profit per (full, if not parity) equity partner.
31 Measured by fee income.
32 Adapted from PwC, *Annual Law Firms' Survey 2020: Embracing Change to Succeed*, www.pwc.co.uk/industries/business-services/law-firms/survey.html.
33 Maybe it is the ongoing impact of the salary war provoked by US firms in London.
34 www.ft.com/content/b593b3cc-a75f-4b6a-8f75-1ad95b18bd38.
35 Qualifying as a solicitor typically involves three or four years of postgraduate study and (salaried) apprenticeship-style training.
36 See also reports of the review of partner profit sharing models away from the lockstep model, which rewards long service and loyalty in the most conservative UK firms.
37 PwC (n 27).
38 Lock-up is the sum value of work undertaken, but not paid for (and in some cases not billed).
39 PwC (n 27).
40 *Ibid.*
41 David Dorion, Law Crossing, "5 Important Qualities Every Lawyer Should Have", www.lawcrossing.com/article/900049695/The-5-Personal-Qualities-needed-to-be-an-Effective-Lawyer/.
42 Arizona State University, National Transactional Clinic, conference hosted by College of Law ASU News (8 June 2010), quoting Professor Thomas H Morsch.
43 The truth is that they will still demand the old skills, but also look for more.
44 For more on this, see S Danegl and MJ Madison, "Innovators Esq: Training the Next Generation of Lawyer Social Entrepreneurs", *University of Missouri-Kansas City Law Review*, vol. 83, p967 (2015).
45 At this point, the temptation to reference *Yes Minister* is irresistible – specifically, Sir Humphrey Appleby's observation that a 'brave' decision was one that would lose the government votes, whereas a 'courageous' one was one that would lose the election. Maybe this has affected lawyers more than we understand...
46 JD Bliss, "Interview: Tim Zagat: From Law to Leisure Guide Empire" (13 March 2007), www.jbblissblog.com/2007/06/interview-tim-z.html.
47 Of the University of Miami School of Law and elsewhere (www.law.miami.edu/faculty/michele-destefano).
48 M DeStefano and G Dobrauz-Saldapenna, *New Suits: Appetite for Disruption in the Legal World* (Stampfli Verlag, 2019).
49 *Ibid*, p93.
50 *Ibid*, p91.
51 Sir Ernest Ryder speaking in March 2011, as quoted by Joshua Rozenberg QC in The Legal Education Forum, "On line courts – will IT work?", https://long-reads.thelegaleducationfoundation.org/.
52 https://remotecourts.org/.
53 https://remotecourts.org/files/Shall%20We%20Have%20a%20Rethink.pdf.
54 [2020] EWCA Civ 503.
55 In February 2021, it was reported that Addleshaw Goddard and Pinsent Masons had both opened new offices, in Paris and Amsterdam respectively. See *Legal Business*, "Revolving doors, Pinsents and Addleshaws plant new flags in Europe as firms make key partner hires", 3 February 2021, www.legalbusiness.co.uk/blogs/revolving-doors-pinsents-and-addleshaws-plant-new-flags-in-europe-as-firms-make-key-partner-hires/?utm_medium=push_notification&utm_source=rss&utm_campaign=rss_VWO+Engage&notification_source=pushcrew_rss.
56 The *FT* Innovative Lawyer Awards continue to celebrate widespread innovation in approaches to client service, operational and business models, as they have done for 25 years, *Financial Times*, "Clients are going digital, and so must the lawyers", 2 October 2020, www.ft.com/content/3a2e9899-2b64-429f-9fa8-878123f3cb84.
57 For example, Keystone Law reported 14 partner-level appointments in November 2020, having already announced 15 joiners in August 2020. *The Global Legal Post* commented: "Keystone's impressive growth is arguably indicative of the increasing popularity of virtual firms". See *The Global Legal Post*, "Keystone Law continues recruitment drive with bumper hiring spree from Clifford Chance and others", 19 August 2020, www.globallegalpost.com/big-stories/keystone-law-continues-recruitment-drive-with-bumper-hiring-spree-from-clifford-chance-and-others-96392289/.
58 Civil Litigation Brief, "Skype hearings and appeals: Court of Appeal are stepping on the gas", 8 April 2020, www.civillitigationbrief.com/2020/04/08/skype-hearings-and-appeals-court-of-appeal-are-stepping-on-the-gas/.
59 Adam Grant, *Think Again* (Virgin Digital, 2021).
60 NHS Website, "Mindfulness", www.nhs.uk/conditions/stress-anxiety-depression/mindfulness/.
61 *APA Dictionary of Psychology*, Second Edition, https://dictionary.apa.org/empathy.
62 *Ibid*.
63 Bar Standards Board, Professional Statement for Barristers, 2016, www.barstandardsboard.org.uk/uploads/assets/a4556161-bd81-448d-874d40f3baaf8fe2/bsbprofessionalstatementandcompetences2016.pdf.

64 Daniel Goleman, *Hot to Help*, 1 March 2008, https://greatergood.berkeley.edu/article/item/hot_to_help.
65 *Ibid.*
66 Harper Lee, *To Kill A Mockingbird* (JP Lippincott, 1960).
67 Talmage Boston, "Who Was Atticus Finch?", *Texas Bar Journal*, Vol 73, No 6, June 2010, 483–487, www.texasbar.com/AM/Template.cfm?Section=Texas_Bar_Journal&Template=/CM/ContentDisplay.cfm&ContentID=9585.
68 Casey Cep, "The Contested Legacy of Atticus Finch: Harper Lee's beloved father figure became a talking point during the Kavanaugh hearings and is now coming to Broadway. Is he still a hero?", *The New Yorker*, 17 December 2018, www.newyorker.com/magazine/2018/12/17/the-contested-legacy-of-atticus-finch.
69 Richard Mullender, Matteo Nicolini, Thomas DC Bennett and Emilia Mickiewicz (eds), *Law and Imagination in Troubled Times: A Legal and Literary Discourse* (Routledge, 2020), p1.
70 Albert Einstein, *On Cosmic Religion: With Other Opinions and Aphorisms* (Dover Publications, 1931), p49.
71 Travis N Turner and Robert H Frantz, "L'Artiste Lawyer: How to Solve Problems with Creative Thinking", *ACC Docket*, March 2013, 36–42, https://uk.practicallaw.thomsonreuters.com/Link/Document/Blob/I42aaa5af0c5511e498db8b09b4f043e0.pdf?targetType=PLC-multimedia&originationContext=document&transitionType=DocumentImage&uniqueId=73c6dae8-9be5-48a5-861d-1973f14e9a89&contextData=%28sc.Default%29&comp=pluk.
72 *Ibid.*
73 Nick Saunders Cho, "The Conversation: A Decade of Innovative Lawyering", *Thomson Reuters*, 27 April 2016, https://blogs.thomsonreuters.com/answerson/conversation-innovative-lawyers-legal-industry/.
74 *Ibid.*
75 Owen Bowcott, "Legal Professional Hits Back at Johnson over 'lefty lawyers' speech", *The Guardian*, 6 October 2020, www.theguardian.com/law/2020/oct/06/legal-profession-hits-back-at-boris-johnson-over-lefty-lawyers-speech.
76 Zohra Nabi, "Priti Patel attacks 'lefty lawyers' and human rights 'do-gooders'", *The Justice Gap*, 6 October 2020, www.thejusticegap.com/priti-patel-attacks-lefty-lawyers-and-human-rights-do-gooders/.
77 *Daily Mail*, front cover, 4 November 2016, www.dailymail.co.uk/news/article-3903436/Enemies-people-Fury-touch-judges-defied-17-4m-Brexit-voters-trigger-constitutional-crisis.html.
78 Amy Bernstein, "COVID-19 Dealt a Blow to Working Women. Can We Emerge Stronger?", *New York Times*, 7 December 2020, www.nytimes.com/2020/12/07/opinion/covid-women-work-careers.html?searchResultPosition=1.
79 Economic Statistics Centre of Excellence, "Estimating the UK population during the pandemic", 14 January 2021, www.escoe.ac.uk/estimating-the-uk-population-during-the-pandemic/.
80 Lanre Bakare, "Government scraps ballet dancer reskilling ad criticised as 'crass': Culture secretary distanced himself from widely mocked poster amid job losses in arts", *The Guardian*, 12 October 2020, www.theguardian.com/politics/2020/oct/12/ballet-dancer-could-reskill-with-job-in-cyber-security-suggests-uk-government-ad.
81 Office of the United Nations High Commissioner for Human Rights, Basic Principles on the Role of Lawyers, adopted by the Eighth United Nations Congress on the Prevention of Crime and the Treatment of Offenders, Havana, Cuba, 27 August to 7 September 1990, www.ohchr.org/EN/ProfessionalInterest/Pages/RoleOfLawyers.aspx.
82 Abby Ohlheiser, "Why 'social justice warrior,' a Gamergate insult, is now a dictionary entry", *Washington Post*, 7 October 2015, www.washingtonpost.com/news/the-intersect/wp/2015/10/07/why-social-justice-warrior-a-gamergate-insult-is-now-a-dictionary-entry/.
83 Eli Wald, "The Economic Downturn and the Legal Profession, Foreword: The Great Recession and the Legal Profession", 78 *Fordham L Rev* 2051, 2052–2052 (2010), https://ir.lawnet.fordham.edu/flr/vol78/iss5/1.
84 Sarah Randazzo, "Big Law Firms Prosper Despite Covid-Impaired Economy", *The Wall Street Journal*, 5 October 2020, www.wsj.com/articles/big-law-firms-prosper-despite-covid-impaired-economy-11601890200.

# About the authors

**Jonathan Fortnam**
Dean, Aston Law School
j.fortnam@aston.ac.uk

Jonathan Fortnam became dean of Aston Law School, College of Business and Social Sciences, Aston University, Birmingham, in 2019 after 30 years' practice experience at Pinsent Masons LLP, 21 of which were as a partner. Jonathan's work at Pinsent Masons focused on corporate litigation (including a term as chief operating officer of the litigation and regulatory team), and on developing award-winning innovation in client relationships (including tools to assess and manage risk), and the firm's approach to responsible business.

**Stuart Weinstein**
Reader in legal risk management, Aston Law School
s.weinstein@aston.ac.uk

Stuart Weinstein is reader in legal risk management at Aston Law School. Stuart was previously general counsel at a global multinational and is contributing editor to Globe Law and Business's series on legal risk management. Stuart served as subject-matter expert to the British Standards Institute Working Group on the development of BS ISO 31022:2020, which provides guidelines for managing the specific challenges of legal risk faced by organisations and is a complementary document to ISO 31000:2018 – Risk Management Guidelines.

# About Globe Law and Business

Globe Law and Business was established in 2005. From the very beginning, we set out to create law books which are sufficiently high level to be of real use to the experienced professional, yet still accessible and easy to navigate. Most of our authors are drawn from Magic Circle and other top commercial firms, both in the UK and internationally.

Our titles are carefully produced, with the utmost attention paid to editorial, design and production processes. We hope this results in high-quality publications that are easy to read, and a pleasure to own. Our titles are also available as ebooks, which are compatible with most desktop, laptop and tablet devices. In 2018 we expanded our portfolio to include journals and Special Reports, available both digitally and in hard-copy format, and produced to the same high standards as our books.

We'd very much like to hear from you with your thoughts and ideas for improving what we offer. Please do feel free to email me at sian@globelawandbusiness.com with your views.

Sian O'Neill
Managing director
Globe Law and Business
www.globelawandbusiness.com

www.ingramcontent.com/pod-product-compliance
Ingram Content Group UK Ltd.
Pitfield, Milton Keynes, MK11 3LW, UK
UKHW050011141125
465057UK00006B/100